THE

PUBLICATIONS

OF THE

THORESBY SOCIETY

ESTABLISHED IN THE YEAR
MDCCCLXXXIX

SECOND SERIES
VOLUME TWO
for 1991

R. D. Chantrell, portrait, artist unknown.

R. D. Chantrell, Architect: His Life and Work in Leeds 1818–1847

by

Christopher Webster, MPhil

THE THORESBY SOCIETY
23 CLARENDON ROAD
LEEDS
1992

ISSN 0082–4232

ISBN 0 900741 27 9

Published by The Thoresby Society
and printed by the University Printing Service
at the University of Leeds

Contents

List of Plates

Preface

The circumstances which led Robert Dennis Chantrell to settle in Leeds in 1819 are not altogether clear; neither are the reasons for his departure in 1846 for semi-retirement in London. Yet during those twenty-seven years much has been recorded about his professional activities in Yorkshire, and for much of that period he could, quite justifiably, have thought of himself as the leading Leeds architect. Indeed, in 1843, the Bishop of Ripon referred to him as 'one of the first architects in all the North of England'. Nevertheless it appears that Leeds soon forgot its 'gifted townsman'. Architectural taste changed quickly, and the work of the next generation of practitioners, like Cuthbert Brodrick and George Corson, must have made Chantrell's work appear old-fashioned. His death in 1872 does not appear to have warranted an obituary in either the local or national press. No private papers have been found, and there were no memoirs or biography on which to draw in the preparation of this study. Instead, material has been gathered from a wide variety of archive sources, covering his public and ecclesiastical commissions, and his dealings with various institutions. In addition, much useful material appeared in the pages of the *Leeds Intelligencer*. Sadly, almost nothing which refers to his private life or personality has been found.

I began my research on Chantrell in the mid 1970s, for an MPhil degree. As the work progressed it became increasingly clear that he was a competent rather than a great architect. His churches of the mid 1840s show much promise, and his theoretical work is of significance in the context of the Early Victorian Gothic Revival; yet it seems his premature retirement precluded his attaining what might otherwise have been national stature. Thus my interest gradually shifted from the study of his designs to a consideration of his professionalism and the wider issues of the beginnings of the architectural profession in the provinces. It is perhaps in this latter context that Chantrell is most worthy of study: much has been written about the careers of his successful metropolitan contemporaries, but relatively little research has been devoted to the provincial practices of the first half of the nineteenth century.

I was fortunate to have had as my MPhil supervisor Professor Derek Linstrum. I shall always be grateful to him for his encouragement and advice, and for sharing with me the fruits of his extensive scholarship.

I would like to record my special thanks also to Andries Van den Abeele. The unexpected arrival of a letter from him in connection with his own research on Chantrell's brothers in Bruges proved to be the beginning of a correspondence – and subsequently friendship – which has now continued for almost a decade. Although we exchanged information, I was the major beneficiary of the arrangement, and sections in this study dealing with Chantrell's early life, family and the Bruges Cathedral commission would have been much thinner without his kind assistance.

I am grateful to George and David Atkinson, Maurice Beresford, Stanley Chadwick, Howard Colvin, John Dunhill, William Elgie, Geoffrey Forster, Terry Friedman, John Goodchild, Hilary Grainger, Ellis Gummer, Malcolm Neeson, Michael Port and Donald Webster for their help in various ways.

Numerous clergy and churchwardens kindly allowed me to inspect their churches and archive material in their care. In addition, I would like to acknowledge the assistance of the staff of the following libraries and archive collections: the Borthwick Institute, York; the Archive Department of the Church Commissioners; the Dean and Chapter Library, York Minster; the Greater London Record Office; the Incorporated Church Building Society; the Library of Lambeth Palace; the West Yorkshire Joint Archive Service (Leeds and Wakefield offices); Leeds City Libraries, Local History Department; University of Leeds, Brotherton Library (Special Collections); the North Yorkshire Records Office; Sir John Soane's Museum; the Society of Antiquaries; the Thoresby Society, Leeds; the West Derbyshire Record Office. To all those who gave me permission to quote from their collections, I am indebted.

Anna Mawson, Joyce Rathbone and Jacqui Marshall produced the original typescript; their patience and diligence were much appreciated. My thanks are due to Joan Kirby and Rosemary Stephens, the Thoresby Society's Honorary Editors, for their painstaking editing of my typescript, and for many helpful suggestions.

CHRISTOPHER WEBSTER
STAFFORDSHIRE UNIVERSITY

Acknowledgements for Plates

I am grateful to the following for permission to reproduce photographs, drawings or documents in their possession: the Borthwick Institute of Historical Research; the Church Commissioners; the Incorporated Church Building Society; Leeds City Libraries; Leeds City Museum; State Archives, Bruges; the Thoresby Society; the Victoria and Albert Museum, Picture Library; West Yorkshire Joint Archive Service (Leeds City Archives).

The remaining photographs are my own.

C.W.

Hon. Editors' Acknowledgements

The publication of this volume has been assisted by grants from the following:

> THE LATE MR STANLEY H. BURTON
> LEEDS AND HOLBECK BUILDING SOCIETY
> THE PAUL MELLON CENTRE FOR STUDIES
>   IN BRITISH ART
> PRAYER BOOK SOCIETY
> THE VICTORIAN SOCIETY
>   (WEST YORKSHIRE BRANCH)

On behalf of the Thoresby Society the Hon. Editors record their thanks for this generous help.

Abbreviations and Short Titles

CBC	Church Building Commission, 1818–1856 (*Church House, Westminster*)
CBC MB	Church Building Commission, Board Meetings Minute Books
CBC BC MB	Church Building Commission, Building Committee Minute Books
CBC SB	Church Building Commission, Surveyor's Books
GLRO	Greater London Record Office (*40 Northampton Row, London EC1 0JU*)
ICBS	Incorporated Church Building Society (*Lambeth Palace Library*)
LCA	Leeds City Archives (West Yorkshire Joint Archive Service, Leeds Office)
LCL	Leeds City Library (Reference Section), Local History Department
LI	*Leeds Intelligencer*
LPCA	Leeds Parish Church Archives (located at Leeds City Archives)
LUL	Leeds University Library
Linstrum	D. Linstrum, *West Yorkshire Architects and Architecture* (1978)
PTh.S	*Publications of the Thoresby Society*
SM	Sir John Soane's Museum, London
TS	Library of the Thoresby Society
Taylor	R. V. Taylor, *Ecclesiae Leodienses* (1875)
Webster	I. C. Webster, 'The Life and Work of R. D. Chantrell, Architect' (MPhil thesis, University of York, 1985)
WYJAS	West Yorkshire Joint Archive Service

CHAPTER I

Introduction

This work explores two areas of study: architectural history and social history. An examination of the career of Robert Dennis Chantrell, perhaps the most important early nineteenth-century architect in Leeds, must also include aspects of the social history of Leeds in this period, since Chantrell's fortunes as an architect were inextricably linked to the interests, aspirations and prosperity of the society for which he worked.

As both architectural and social history, the subject has a significance beyond the study of Leeds. Chantrell belonged to the first generation of metropolitan-trained architects to settle in the provinces, introducing new standards of professional competence, largely unknown to earlier generations of builder-architects. His career therefore represents a significant case study of these early attempts to establish professional attitudes in the practice of architecture outside the metropolis. The physical changes taking place in industrial centres like Leeds, where Chantrell lived between 1819 and 1846, were the result of their development into major manufacturing towns. In Leeds, as elsewhere, the thriving local economy generated significant wealth for those fortunate enough to belong to the upper middle class, who had ample money to finance the erection of new houses, and to subscribe to public or religious buildings intended both to ornament the town and improve its facilities. Amongst the most significant developments taking place nationally in the erection of new buildings at this time were initiatives in church building, and ecclesiastical commissions were to account for the bulk of Chantrell's professional employment.

In order to put Chantrell's career in Leeds into a wider context, this introduction will examine briefly three aspects of the c. 1815–50 era: the growth of Leeds; the emergence of the architectural profession in the town; and the events which led to a rapid increase in church building.

The growth of Leeds

Chantrell's residence in Leeds from 1819 to 1846 saw the population of the town approximately double,[1] and there was a similar increase

---

[1] Based on the census reports, quoted in *A History of Modern Leeds*, ed. D. Fraser (Manchester, 1980), p.48.

in its housing stock, 8,795 new houses being built between the
censuses of 1821 and 1841.[2] However, whilst the erection of dwelling
houses, industrial buildings, warehouses, shops, and public houses[3]
brought plenty of work for the building tradesmen, it did not, in
most cases, provide employment for architects; where designs for
these types of buildings existed on paper, they were more likely to
have been supplied by the builders or surveyors.[4] This study is
concerned rather with the erection of those buildings – religious and
public – which were likely to require the services of an architect.

Professor Beresford has usefully pointed out that the increasing
number of public and religious buildings was catalogued by the
cartographers of Leeds: Netlam and Francis Giles' plan of 1815 lists
forty-eight churches, chapels and public buildings; Charles Fowler
extended this list to fifty-four in his map of 1821, and in his revised
editions of 1826, 1831 and 1844 the numbers were eighty-two, 124
and 181 respectively.[5]

The increase in the numbers of religious and public buildings can
also be gauged by noting the 'invitations to tender' advertised in the
pages of the newspapers. In the early 1820s there were about two or
three per year, but by the mid 1830s this had risen to five or six. To
these figures can be added notices in the papers of newly completed
buildings. Thus in the six years 1834–39 the *Intelligencer* made
reference to at least forty-five new religious or public buildings –
including seventeen nonconformist chapels – that were erected
within the town.[6]

During the eighteenth century, the most significant group of new
buildings was the various cloth halls, in which the merchants
conducted their business. By the turn of the century, however,

---

[2] *Ibid.*, p.73.

[3] See Maurice Beresford, *East End, West End: the face of Leeds during urbanisation, 1684–1846* (*PTh.S*, LX and LXI, 1988) for a full account of the physical development of Leeds during this period.

[4] Dividing building types between those that did or did not provide employment to architects is problematic and there are few rules. So far as Leeds was concerned in this period, all the new churches were architect-designed whereas, so far as the author is aware, none of the very large number of working-class housing developments was, but see F. Trowell, 'Speculative housing development in the suburb of Headingley, Leeds, 1838–1914', *PTh.S*, LIX (1985), 50–118, for a full discussion. However, for other building types the picture is less clear: an individual shop was unlikely to be an architect's work, a row of shops might be and a market almost certainly would be designed by an architect.

[5] Fraser, pp.108–09.

[6] The public building activities in Leeds during this period are described and put into the context of developments within the West Riding in K. Grady, *The Georgian Public Buildings of Leeds and the West Riding* (*PTh.S*, LXII, 1989).

buildings began to appear purposely to accommodate those fashionable leisure activities which were now no longer the sole preserve of such places as London, Bath or York. In 1771 the theatre in Hunslet Lane was opened,[7] the spacious and elegant Assembly Rooms were built between 1775 and 1777,[8] and in 1792 to these was added the Music Hall in Albion Street.[9]

The attempt of Leeds to compete with her more fashionable neighbours in terms of 'provincial enlightenment' was yet a further stimulus to new buildings. In 1808 Thomas Johnson designed elegant new premises for the Leeds Library in Commercial Street.[10] A new Philosophical and Literary Society was formed in 1819, followed by a Mechanics' Institute in 1825 and a Literary Institute in 1834.[11] Bridging the gap between business and education was Calvert's Museum of Natural History which was opened in 1827 as a commercial venture, sited appropriately in Commercial Street.[12] In addition to these, a number of schools were built in the early nineteenth century.

Clearly Leeds was expanding and acquiring new public buildings as a tangible sign of its prosperity and rising status. However, the undisputed wealth which resulted from commercial successes could not, by itself, produce the sophisticated quality of life to be found in the old-established county towns or fashionable resorts. A directory of 1817 contained the following unflattering report:

> With the exception of those arts which have an immediate reference to commerce and manufacture, philosophical researches are not much cultivated in Leeds, still less do literary pursuits engage the attention of its inhabitants . . . a society for the discussion of literary and moral subjects was formed in 1793,[13] but after varying success was entirely given up . . . Fine Arts are not much better. The Northern Society for the Encouragement of the Arts was formed in 1808 but after three exhibitions has given up . . .[14].

[7] It was similar to, although a little larger than, the theatre at Richmond (Linstrum, p.269). See also J. Copley, 'The Theatre in Hunslet Lane', I and II, *PTh.S*, LIV (1976), 65–77, 196–208.

[8] Linstrum, p.379.

[9] P. Robinson, *Leeds Old and New* (Leeds, 1926), p.44.

[10] Linstrum, p.379.

[11] The latter two institutions merged in 1842. W. White, *History, Gazetteer and Directory of the West Riding of Yorkshire* . . . 2 vols (Sheffield, 1837), I, 527.

[12] W. Parson and W. White, *Directory of the Borough of Leeds* . . . (Leeds, 1830), p.215.

[13] This should be 1783.

[14] E. Baines, *Directory, General and Commercial of* . . . *Leeds* (Leeds, 1826), p.41.

Perhaps the uncertain success which greeted the numerous initiatives in the provision of cultural and recreational facilities in Leeds can, to a considerable extent, be explained by the rise of the middle and lower classes and the corresponding retreat of the upper classes from the town's activities.

> Though Leeds was formerly connected with some of the principal families of the West Riding, some of whom made it their place of residence, others sustained offices in its Corporation and others interested themselves in the transactions of its affairs, it has long been totally abandoned by the aristocracy. Three distinguished noble families reside within a few miles of it [at Harewood, Temple Newsam and Methley] but are seldom to be seen in its streets; the independence of manufacturing wealth being inconsistent with both the pride of dignity and rank.[15]

The *Leeds Intelligencer* dutifully recorded the activities of the local aristocracy; its 'Local Intelligence' column invariably began with such items as a report of Lord Grantham's fête at Newby Hall,[16] or details of the nuptials of Mr William Lane-Fox and Miss Douglas, granddaughter of the Earl of Harewood, which led to enhanced Christmas festivities at Bramham and Harewood.[17] Even news of the Harewood foxhounds was respectfully placed at the top of the local news column. But although the *Intelligencer* chronicled the activities of the nobility and gentry, there is no mention of any of them even visiting the town, or taking part in its affairs in this period.

As building activities increased in the centre of the town, so there was a corresponding development in the suburbs. Cossins's map of the town of 1725 shows that there were houses in Briggate with gardens at the front and orchards at the rear. This gives some idea of the rural, market-town character which Leeds still possessed at this time. Half a century later, little change had taken place; the parish church, St John's, and the Mixed Cloth Hall roughly marked the extent of the town and there were still several open spaces within this triangle. The newly built Infirmary was surrounded by fields

---

[15] W. White, *History, Gazetteer and Directory of the West Riding of Yorkshire*, p.496.
[16] *LI*, 25 Aug. 1818.
[17] *Ibid.*, 5 Jan. 1818.

and there was little development on the south side of the river.[18] However, the 1760s saw the beginning of a new development to the west of the town in Park Row and East Parade, that extended, by the end of the century, to Park Place and Park Square. The wealthy merchants who had earlier lived in Briggate or near the parish church now moved either out of the town altogether, or at least to the more fashionable and spacious western fringe, as the town's expansion made their earlier homes less desirable. The most prestigious part of this expansion, begun in 1788, was around Park Square, which had the added éclat of its own church when St Paul's was completed in 1793. '[In Park Place] are the elegant new houses fronting towards the fields. This is esteemed one of the most pleasant and healthy situations in Leeds . . .', stated a directory of 1797.[19]

No doubt as a result of the success of this scheme, several other areas were laid out for squares or regular terraces in the late eighteenth and early nineteenth centuries. Robert Denison's house in Town End was for sale in 1791, and its estate was described in the following year as 'capable of being converted into one or more Rows of elegant Buildings . . . or otherwise of forming a handsome street . . .'.[20] Watson and Pritchett were responsible for designs for laying out Hanover Square in 1823[21] and as late as 1840, John Clark produced a design for Woodhouse Square.[22] In these developments, Leeds followed the fashions of London and Edinburgh squares. However, none of these later schemes came anywhere near to completion. One reason for this was that the western side of the town had also been chosen as the site for an extensive new mill: 'Besides the river in the fields called Bene-Ing is the woollen mill belonging to Messrs Wormald, Fountain and Gott. It is the most complete and extensive in the town and neighbourhood . . .'[23]; another reason was a growing belief that the villa was the ideal type of residence.[24]

---

[18] R. Sayer and J. Bennett, *A Plan of Leeds*, published 1775.

[19] G. Wright, *A History of the Town and Parish of Leeds* (Leeds, 1797), p. 25.

[20] Linstrum, p. 102.

[21] TS, Drawing Box A. Tenders for three houses were advertised in *LI*, 13 Jan. 1825. See also Beresford, *East End, West End*, pp. 332–33, 341–42.

[22] Linstrum, p. 105. Tenders were advertised for houses in the square in *LI*, 1 March 1845. See also Beresford, *East End, West End*, pp. 335–36.

[23] Wright, p. 13.

[24] In this respect Leeds was following a national trend. The large number of 'pattern books' devoted to 'villa residences' which appeared from *c.* 1800 is evidence of the popularity of this type of house. For the development of the villa in Leeds, see Beresford, *East End, West End*, esp. pp. 307–09, 319–29, 335–47.

The villa was essentially a modest-sized detached house set in a garden of a few acres. Obviously, such sites could not be found in the centre of the town, or around a new square; and this fact, coupled with the increasing dirt of even the western suburbs, prompted those who could afford the cost to move to the more pleasant environs to the north and west of the town. An account of the town published in 1797 stated, 'Little Woodhouse . . . has of late years been made chosen of by some of the wealthy inhabitants of Leeds for building their country houses and the whole villa[ge] has an appearance of superior elegance'. The author goes on to say,

> . . . from the brow of the hill beyond Little Woodhouse we have a true prospect of the beautiful and fertile Vale of Aire with the river flowing through it. Scattered villas and the Gentlemen's seats exhibit a contrast of industry and opulent independence whilst the improved state of the country and the high degree of cultivation call forth a sentiment of gratitude to the author of nature who has graciously fitted this world for the convenience and happiness of mankind . . .[25]

In Leeds, the prestige of the villa received a significant boost when Benjamin Gott purchased an estate at Armley in 1803. Gott was the owner of Bean Ing Mill, and one of the wealthiest and most influential of the Leeds industrialists. At Armley, he transformed the modest late eighteenth-century house, employing Robert Smirke as architect and Humphry Repton as landscape gardener, and filled the completed house with an impressive collection of works of art. This same pair of designers was also employed by John Blayds, a Leeds banker, to remodel the hall and park at Oulton, about five miles south-east of the town.[26] Gott and Blayds were exceptional; none of their fellow townsmen could match their patronage, but, within their means, they set the fashion for others to follow.

A map of 1806[27] shows that the town had expanded in every direction; east past the parish church towards Quarry Hill, on the south side of the river, and north-west along Woodhouse Lane.

[25] Wright, p. 34.

[26] See G. Worsley, 'Oulton Hall', in *Country Life*, 17 Sept. 1987, pp. 146–49. Repton was first consulted in 1809, and Smirke's alterations to the hall were probably carried out in the early 1820s. See also V. M. E. Lovell, 'Benjamin Gott of Armley House, Leeds, 1762–1840: patron of the arts', *PTh.S*, LIX (1985), 180–83.

[27] John Heaton, publisher, *Plan of the town of Leeds with its modern improvements*, engraved by C. Livesey (Leeds, 1806).

Similarly, a map of 1815[28] shows expansion in the same areas but on a greater scale. The south-east section, Richmond Hill, had seen much growth since 1806, as had St James's Street off Woodhouse Lane.

The rapid expansion of the eastern and southern sections was in response to the increasing number of working-class families who were lured to the town to work in the factories. 'Westerly winds are most prevalent and drive the columns of smoke arising from the numerous manufactories to the eastern part of the town . . . the New Bank is the most populous part of the suburbs . . . on the eastern side of the Aire.'[29] Leeds was thus neatly divided between the west for the middle classes and east for the working classes. In the early nineteenth century, the town extended about two miles from east to west and a little over one mile from north to south.[30]

Here, to Leeds, Robert Dennis Chantrell came in 1819: he could not have chosen a more propitious time or place to have begun an architectural career.

The architectural profession in Leeds
The physical expansion of Leeds during the nineteenth century was, to a considerable extent, the continuation of a pattern already begun, but whereas the development of the town in the earlier period was largely undertaken without the presence of what might be termed 'professional' architects, increasingly after 1815 it is possible to identify those to whom such a term could be applied; men who had been thoroughly trained to uphold rigorous standards of competence and behaviour in their business affairs and, for the most part, did not combine the practice of architecture with building, supplying materials, surveying or any of the other associated trades.

Before *c.*1815 the employment of architects had been largely confined to country houses; there were relatively few urban commissions. Thus, in assessing Chantrell's career in Leeds, it must be recognised that he was among the first members of this emerging profession to be based in an industrial centre and to be employed mainly on urban, rather than rural, commissions. He was, therefore, in the position of having to create a demand for services which had

[28] Netlam and Francis Giles, surveyors, *Plan of the town of Leeds and its environs* (Leeds, 1815).
[29] E. Baines, *Directory, General and Commercial of. . . Leeds*, p.29.
[30] W. White, *West Riding Directory* (Leeds, 1857), p.478.

hitherto largely gone unrecognised, rather than respond to a clearly defined need for these professional services.

However, Chantrell was not the town's first architect. Although the directory of 1798 does not include anyone so described, there were local men capable of producing a design. For instance, John Moxson (1700–82) was responsible for the Coloured or Mixed Cloth Hall in the 1750s, William Johnson (d. 1795) probably designed the 'New' White Cloth Hall and the Assembly Rooms, both in the 1770s, and William's son, Thomas (d. 1814), designed a number of buildings, including the Leeds Library in 1808. But it is important to recognise that these men probably did not see themselves primarily as 'architects': Moxson held the position of surveyor of the highways in Leeds, William Johnson was agent to Lord Irwin at Temple Newsam, and Thomas Johnson perhaps acted extensively as a land or estate agent.

The *Commercial Directory* of 1814 lists four architects: Benjamin Jackson, Thomas Johnson, William Lawrance and Thomas Taylor. However, the apparently sudden appearance of this quartet is not entirely due to a dramatic increase in the demand for architectural services; in part it reflects the extent to which architecture had come to be regarded as an independent activity. It is clear that, earlier, a number of Leeds craftsmen supplied designs for the buildings on which they worked, but would not have thought of themselves primarily as architects. It was, perhaps, their aspiration towards a higher social status that prompted some craftsmen subsequently to advertise their services as 'architects', although it is probable that their day-to-day pattern of work changed very little. For instance, Lawrance is known to have built, and almost certainly designed, a number of houses in Park Square in the 1790s, yet in the 1798 *Directory* he appears as a 'joiner and cabinet maker'.[31] However, in 1807 he publicly informed

> . . . his numerous Friends that he has declined the Business of Joiner and Carpenter . . . [and] begs Permission to offer his Services to the Public as an ARCHITECT, SURVEYOR, and VALUER OF BUILDINGS; and to inform them, that he intends carrying on the Business of a RAFF-MERCHANT on his premises in Simpson's Fold, and shall be happy to receive a Share of their Commands.[32]

[31] J. Ryley, *The Leeds Directory* (Leeds, 1798), p.33.
[32] *Leeds Mercury*, 17 Jan. 1807, quoted in Linstrum, p.33.

The advertisement also illustrates the common practice of the period of combining architecture with other business interests.

Benjamin Jackson appears to have been more active as an estate agent,[33] although a small number of designs by him are known. For example, he was responsible for the uniform fronted houses in St Mark's Terrace, Leeds of *c*.1832,[34] and an unexecuted scheme for the proposed Leeds workhouse in 1835.[35]

The town's first truly 'professional' architect was Thomas Taylor (*c*.1778–1826), who, having undergone a thorough training in architecture, did not find it necessary, or perhaps did not think it appropriate, to combine the practice of architecture with estate agency or dealing in building materials. Having spent five years working for a London builder, Taylor subsequently passed eight years in the office of James Wyatt. His exhibits at the Royal Academy from 1792 to 1811 show that he was a skilled draughtsman. In *c*.1810 he settled in Leeds, and on securing the prestigious commission to design the new Court House there in 1811, he placed the following advertisement in the *Intelligencer*:

> . . . the NEW COURT HOUSE . . . with his other Engagements in the County will render him stationary in Leeds, where he will be happy to receive the Commands of those who might have Occasion for his Professional Services, in which he flatters himself enabled to give every Satisfaction, as during a Period of Eight Years Practice under Mr James Wyatt, the present Surveyor-General . . . he is enabled to calculate Estimates upon an unerring Principle, and further trusts from having made careful Studies of all the superior French Buildings, he is enabled to arrange Architectural Decorations in a superior Style; Specimens of which may be seen in several distinguished Mansions in this Neighbourhood.[36]

Taylor's announcement came at almost the same time as Smirke was remodelling Armley House for Benjamin Gott, and setting a new standard of Classical elegance in the town. It was a standard with which the purely local 'architects' could not compete, but Taylor's background and professionalism enabled him to work

[33] On a number of occasions he placed advertisements in the *LI* offering land for sale and buildings for sale or to rent, e.g., 3 Aug. 1818, 2 Aug. 1832, 5 Oct. 1833.
[34] *LI*, 31 May 1832.
[35] *Ibid.*, 14 March 1835.
[36] *Ibid.*, 9 Sept. 1811.

successfully with the increasingly discriminating patrons of the area. His professional success made it all the more necessary for the indigenous 'architects' to maintain alternative sources of income to supplement their fees from designing.

It was nine years after Taylor settled in Leeds that Chantrell arrived. Whether Chantrell knew of Taylor's success in the town, and saw it as a model for his own career, can only be a matter for speculation. Clearly he believed that the expansion of the town and its surrounding area offered enough work to sustain two 'professional' architects.

Men like Taylor and Chantrell slowly revolutionised the practice of architecture in the provinces. Through them, and those of their pupils who eventually set up in practice, the new professionalism in provincial architecture flourished. By 1853, only seven years after Chantrell left Leeds, there were no fewer than twenty-two architects practising in the town.[37]

The division which certainly existed in the first half of the nineteenth century between industrial wealth and landowning wealth manifested itself in the way in which these two groups patronized architects. The rapid growth in urban building activity was paralleled by the country house commissions, which, however, were offered only rarely to local architects; usually they went to prestigious London-based practitioners. For instance, Bretton Hall was extended by Jeffry Wyatt in c.1815; Methley Hall was substantially remodelled by Anthony Salvin in 1830–36; Decimus Burton enlarged Grimston Park in 1840 and for the modernisation of Harewood, Sir Charles Barry was employed. Conversely, new buildings in Leeds in this period were rarely designed by a non-resident architect. Although architects from London and elsewhere in the provinces submitted designs for many of the public and ecclesiastical commissions, the Leeds building committees usually selected locally produced schemes. Only in the 1840s did external architects begin to breach this local monopoly.[38]

Church building after 1818

Ecclesiastical commissions were to dominate Chantrell's career and he came to see himself – and was seen by others – as an expert in

[37] W. White, *Directory and Gazetteer of Leeds* . . . (first edn Leeds, 1853; repr. Newton Abbot, 1969), p.61.

[38] For instance, J. M. Derrick was chosen to design Holy Cross Church in 1842, and Scott and Moffatt were engaged for St Andrew's in 1843.

this sphere of professional activity. In 1820 there were fourteen churches within the parish of Leeds: the parish church; four other churches within the town; and nine in the suburbs.[39] The majority of these had been in existence for a considerable time, and only one, St Paul's in Park Square (1791–94), had been built within the previous thirty years. However, within the next thirty years, to 1850, sixteen new churches were built,[40] and by 1872, a further twenty-two were added.[41]

This rapid increase was part of a national movement ushered in by the Church Building Act of 1818 which aimed at providing Anglican churches to accommodate a hugely expanded urban population whose needs had been hitherto totally neglected. One million pounds was provided for the Act's Commissioners to erect new churches, this soon being increased by half as much again in 1824.[42]

But the quality of ecclesiastical architecture left much to be desired. The generally high standard of the privately commissioned secular architecture in this period is, to a considerable degree, attributable to the informed and discriminating taste of the patronage. However, in many cases, the churches of the early nineteenth century were commissioned by committees whose members had only a modest knowledge of, or interest in, aesthetic matters. The result was that often second-rate architects were left to work without critical scrutiny from their patrons. Even the congregations for whom the churches were being built were, in many instances, uninterested in the proposed buildings; in some places they were openly hostile. The situation was far removed from the zeal and communal involvement in church building to be found in the middle ages, the period whose style and godliness the early nineteenth-century church building movement hoped to revive. The problem

---

[39] Taylor, p.62.

[40] This figure is arrived at by extracting material from Taylor, pp.62–66 and adding to this the new churches at Kirkstall, Holbeck and Headingley.

[41] Taylor, p.66.

[42] 58 Geo III, cap.545. The Revd H. Roberson, who paid for the erection of a new church at Liversedge (1812–16), had written a lengthy prospectus, in which he observed, 'The difficulties which present themselves to an individual, or a number of private persons, who might wish to build a church will be strongly felt by every person acquainted with business of this nature. The sum of money requisite is very considerable; and the necessary Arrangements are attended with trouble and inconveniences, which discourage the well-disposed from making those attempts, which, under different circumstances, they would be glad to venture upon' (F. Beckwith, *Thomas Taylor, Regency Architect* (*PTh.S*, Monograph I, 1949), pp.93–94). These problems were considerably eased by the Church Building Act.

was also compounded by shortage of money. The Act told its Commissioners that they were to build on the plans they considered most suitable for providing 'a proper accommodation for the largest number at the least expense',[43] and allowed a maximum of £20,000 to be spent on each church. However, such a sum would allow only fifty churches to be built and to some it seemed an unrealistically small amount when compared with the cost of recent London churches; St Marylebone approximately £60,000[44] and St Pancras £70,000.[45] The 'attached' architects, John Soane, John Nash and Smirke, were asked for advice to which Soane replied that a church to hold 2,000 would cost £33,000[46] and that, 'the largest churches cannot be built without the requisite attention to their character and durability, for a less sum than £30,000'.[47] The fact that by the late 1820s quite large churches were being built for between £3,000 and £4,000,[48] and small ones for about £1,000,[49] gives some idea of the extent to which economy had come to dominate the designing of churches. Indeed the Commissioners' principal concern, when assessing the merits of a particular design, appears to have been the cost of the proposed building in relation to the number of seats it contained. If this was satisfactory their surveyor then had to consider whether the proposed method of construction would produce a suitably durable building. On the issue of style and decoration, the Commissioners made few demands, but at the same time offered little guidance. The Order in Council, by which the Act was administered stated only that 'In every building to be erected under the authority of the Board, the character be preserved, both externally and internally, of an ecclesiastical edifice for divine worship according to the rites of the United Church of England and Ireland'.[50] Certainly decorative details and ornament were considered as dispensable items in the quest for economy, and it was sometimes those features which are essential for the ultimate visual success of a Gothic building which were jettisoned in the initial attempt to reduce costs to an acceptable level. In Chantrell's

[43] M. H. Port, *Six Hundred New Churches* (1961), p.24.

[44] *Ibid.*, p.31.

[45] B. F. L. Clarke, *Church Builders of the Nineteenth Century* (Newton Abbot, 1969), p.25.

[46] Port, p.39.

[47] *Ibid.*, p.40.

[48] For instance Chantrell's St Matthew's, Holbeck, held 1,200 worshippers and cost £3,734 18s. 4½d. (CBC Holbeck file, no. 17,593.)

[49] ICBS, 2028 (Pool): Chantrell's estimate for a new chapel at Pool, to hold 200 worshippers, was a mere £308.

[50] Quoted in Port, p.31.

design for a new church at Holmbridge, near Huddersfield, he included drawings showing the church with and without a spire. Its omission, he had calculated, would reduce the cost from £1,690 to £1,540.[51]

The Commissioners appear to have had no preference for either the Gothic or Classical style and left this to local preferences. However, the great majority of early nineteenth-century churches, whether paid for by the Commissioners or otherwise, were Gothic, and the Classical ones tended to be concentrated in London. One point in favour of Gothic was the belief that it was the cheaper style, not requiring an expensive, and unnecessary, portico. Thomas Taylor went as far as to produce comparative costs for the two styles. With a naïvety typical of the period, he felt that the major difference between the two styles lay in the windows, and showed that Gothic windows were cheaper than 'the modern style'.[52] A further reason for using Gothic was that the majority of people saw it as the traditional style for church building and the one which would, most readily, produce the desired pietistic emotion. 'The Gothic style should be used . . . when one considers the effect of that style of architecture in exciting a degree of solemnity which modern buildings fail to inspire.'[53] Anglican worship was not radically different from that of the nonconformists at this time, and the internal layout dictated by the services of the two denominations were similar. However, supporters of the Established Church considered it important that their new churches should not be mistaken for dissenting chapels and, further, that the churches should be more dignified and 'obviously religious' than those of the nonconformists. So, despite the calls for economy, it was essential that the new churches contained enough ornament for this desired visual superiority. However, had funds been unlimited, anything approaching a facsimile of a medieval church would have been criticised as suggesting popery, and the sublime effect created in some of the medieval cathedrals was thought to be positively dangerous, for it might have resulted in undesirable 'enthusiasm'.[54]

---

[51] WYJAS, Wakefield office: Holmbridge Parish Records, no. 87.

[52] Taylor's calculations are given in full in Beckwith, p. 92. However, it is surprising that Taylor, as one of the more skilled of the architects using the Gothic style, appears not to have recognised that there were much more fundamental differences between successful designs in these two styles.

[53] *LI*, 2 Feb. 1818. This appears as part of a letter which goes on to state that financial savings can be made by using the Gothic style rather than Classicism. The letter was sent anonymously but its contents suggest Taylor's authorship.

[54] For a full discussion of the implications of 'enthusiasm' in the early nineteenth century, see K. Clark, *The Gothic Revival* (1975), pp. 100–01.

Given these somewhat disparate requirements, a form of church evolved quickly which was an orthodox Protestant auditory church in a style that was nominally Gothic. The superficial medievalism made it appear more reverent than a dissenting chapel while the absence of a long chancel and transepts avoided any suggestion of Catholicism. In essence this model was based on the plan evolved by Wren and developed by Gibbs, but in the early nineteenth century the Baroque elements were replaced by Gothic ones. This presented yet another problem for the architects; few of them were familiar with the principles and details of the Gothic style. Almost without exception, the older architects of this period had, for years, designed exclusively in styles derived from Classical antiquity, and the younger architects had been trained to follow the pattern set by their seniors. Furthermore, the illustrated architectural literature of the period offered relatively little help to the would-be Gothicist as the subject had received scant attention in an age which had concentrated its archaeological activity in Italy and Greece and had left the great English abbeys and cathedrals largely unexplored.

Thus the architects employed on these churches found themselves working in the most unfavourable circumstances; they were required to design the buildings quickly, cheaply, in an unfamiliar style and with little clear guidance from their patrons. These factors would surely have tested even the leading architects of the two earlier organised church building programmes, Wren and Hawksmoor. The response to these problems by the principal architects after 1818 was unanimous; they expressed little interest in church building. They continued to devote their professional activities to the more familiar milieu of secular commissions, and were content to let the numerous ecclesiastical commissions, with all their attendant problems, go to ambitious young architects or the less talented members of their own generation. Denied the benefit of the leading architectural minds of the period, the less experienced and the less able were left to attempt an architectural solution to a design problem which history has shown to have been, almost certainly, insoluble.

CHAPTER 2

Early Life, Training and the
Foundations of a Career

Notwithstanding Robert Dennis Chantrell's important family connections in Belgium, the preceding three generations, at least, were English. His great-grandfather Thomas Chantrell died in Salisbury and his great-grandmother Mary (née Speakman) died in London.[1] Their son Robert (1734–1811) was born in Oxford. A grocer by trade, his wife, Dinah Messman (1735–1807), was born in London. The couple had three children – Thomas (1762–1830), Robert junior (1765–1840), and Mary (1777–1847). The birthplace of Thomas and Mary is not known but Robert was born in London, and perhaps the family lived there. Hitherto of the lower middle class, it is with Robert junior, father of Robert Dennis, the architect, that the family's status begins to rise. Chantrell's connection with Newington probably originated in his marriage to Mary Ann Dennis (1776–1829), who was born there, and whose property in Crown Row, Walworth (in the Parish of Newington) thus came into the possession of the Chantrell family. In the early years of their marriage, Robert and Mary led a peripatetic existence as the birthplaces of their children indicate. Their first child, Robert Dennis, was born in Newington in January 1793 but they were living in Ostende in 1794 when Mary Ann was born. Probably as a result of the onset of the war with France they returned to Newington where George was born on 12 August 1795. They do not appear in the Newington rate books at this date, but in 1797 and 1798 Robert was paying rates on the tenth property in Crown Row. He appears in a directory of 1799 where he is recorded as living in East Street, Walworth, but he is not listed in the rate books as living anywhere in the parish in that year. The family had, in fact, moved to Hanover, then a British possession, and they were in Ritzbuttel in August 1799 for the birth of Louise, and in Cuxhaven in 1801 for the birth of William. In 1803 Hanover was occupied by the French so the family returned to Ostende where Suzannah was born later that

---

[1] For sources of information about Chantrell's forebears and their places of residence, see Webster, pp. 29–35.

year. Finally, they arrived in Bruges in 1805, and their youngest child, Emilie Sophie, was born there on 3 November of that year. Robert and Mary made their home in Bruges and died there in 1840 and 1829 respectively.

It was, no doubt, Robert's business interests which had kept the family moving about. In settling in Bruges he became one of a number of English entrepreneurs who chose to make the city their home and commercial base since it offered considerable scope to anyone wishing to develop business interests at this time.[2] Robert appears in the Bruges directories, listed usually as a 'commissionaire' or occasionally as a 'proprietaire'; he is known to have had extensive interests in the shipping, forwarding, importing and exporting of goods,[3] including works of art.[4]

By 1805, when the family settled in Bruges, Robert Dennis would have been twelve and he had already seen more of Europe than most men would have done in a lifetime. In about 1800[5] his father had begun to collect works of art so he would have grown up with paintings and drawings, and probably acquired some of his father's enthusiasm for the visual arts. However, Robert's interest in art was not confined to collecting: works of art were among the items imported and exported by him. Despite the blockade, he was one of a number of dealers engaged in the profitable business of buying art cheaply on the war-ravaged Continent, and exporting it to England. His business interests flourished and some of the wealth he acquired was devoted to the expansion of his own art collection. The annual directories for Bruges note that he possessed a 'cabinet de peintures',[6] and for a public exhibition in 1837 he loaned seven of his paintings. He was also a benefactor of the Academy of Painting and Architecture in Bruges.[7] On his death his collection was auctioned and numbered 174 lots.[8] Such interest was there in the paintings that the sale was preceded by a two-day public exhibition

[2] A. Van den Abeele, 'Entrepreneurs brugeois au XIX siècle: George et William Chantrell', *Bulletin Trimestriel du Credit Communal de Belgique*, 146 (Oct. 1983), p.239.

[3] *Ibid.*, p.240.

[4] Van den Abeele, p.240.

[5] The sale catalogue of Robert's collection of paintings of 1840 notes that the owner had spent forty years in forming the collection.

[6] Ex inf. Andries Van den Abeele.

[7] *Ibid.*

[8] Van de Muser Library, Bruges [Sale Catalogue]: this lists only paintings. It seems unlikely that Robert did not also possess drawings and prints which perhaps were disposed of in a separate sale.

of the collection in the '*grande salle*' of the Town Hall.[9] A translation of the introduction in the catalogue begins: 'The collection of pictures of Mr Robert Chantrell is too well known in the country and abroad for it to be necessary to enter into detail here of the merits of the majority of the canvases which compose this collection . . . '.[10]

Robert Dennis was the only one of Robert's children to leave Bruges,[11] and although subsequently he paid several visits to the city, his family was of little direct relevance in the development of his architectural career. However, it is clear that he inherited his father's interest in the arts and, since he began his architectural training at the age of fourteen, it is almost certain that parental influence would have been important in his choice of career. Since Robert Chantrell had a deep interest in the visual arts as a collector and connoisseur, yet devoted his working life to the more prosaic activities of trade and commerce, it is not altogether surprising that he should have favoured architecture as an appropriate profession for his eldest son. The choice of John Soane in London as the tutor of the son of a Bruges entrepreneur is, perhaps, more surprising. The explanation is almost certainly that Soane was one of Chantrell's clients for continental works of art; a business relationship existed between these two men in 1820,[12] but whether it existed before Robert Dennis had become Soane's pupil is not clear. It is, however, the most plausible explanation and it is known that several of Robert Dennis's fellow pupils were the sons of Soane's friends or business

---

[9] *Ibid.*, p.1.

[10] *Ibid.*, p.3. The catalogue notes that the collection is composed of works of the Dutch, Flemish, Italian and French schools and includes examples by Breugel, Cuyp, Van Dyck, Greuze, twelve Van Oust (which secured high prices), Poussin and forty-five oil sketches on paper, by Rubens.

[11] Many members of the family subsequently attained positions of importance in the province, see F. Koller, *Annuaire des Familles Patriciennes de Belgique* (Brussels, 1941), II, pp.68–70. Ironically, and probably as a result of his leaving Bruges, Robert Dennis became 'forgotten', and Koller fails to note his existence in the list of Robert's children.

[12] Robert Chantrell wrote to Soane 16 May 1820, 'I have lately been so fortunate as to acquire by purchase 40 sketches in oil colours by Rubens on paper. I have also acquired some other good paintings by good masters which I shall take the liberty of showing you in the course of a few months when I hope to visit your city. I beg leave to tender my best services here . . .'. The letter goes on to say that a Bruges artist (?) Mr Deillenlemeerter [this is probably Joseph De Meulemeester (1771–1836)] will soon have for sale sets of engravings after drawings from the Vatican which Chantrell would 'submit' to Soane for 'inspection': SM, Private Correspondence, xv, A, 32. It seems unlikely that the Rubens sketches were sold, as the principal item in the 1840 sale was a set of 45 Rubens oil sketches.

acquaintances.[13] Whatever the reason, the decision to select Soane as Chantrell's teacher was a most fortunate one for the boy. Soane usually had only four or five pupils at any one time and these privileged young men enjoyed what was almost certainly the best architectural education available in England.[14] Soane was undoubtedly the leader of the profession in this period and the pupils had the opportunity to observe him at work over a number of years; he was considered a dedicated teacher, and the year before Chantrell entered his office had been appointed professor of architecture at the Royal Academy, an appointment which he was to hold for thirty years. Moreover, Soane held firm views about professional standards at a time when such matters were of little interest to the majority of his contemporaries; it can be assumed that he instilled the same standards in his pupils, and thus included with their theoretical training a thorough grounding in office practice, estimating and accounting, as well as a sense of professional integrity. In addition, there were educational advantages in simply working at 13 Lincoln's Inn Fields, Soane's remarkable London home and office, over a number of years. The extensive museum, library and drawings collection, plus the constant opportunities to engage in conversation with others who were committed to architecture, must have been significant factors in the pupils' development.

Chantrell's indentures were signed on 14 January 1807, shortly after his fourteenth birthday. The document states that the apprenticeship is to operate for seven years (to 14 January 1814), and that Soane is to provide his pupil with 'board, lodgings and wearing apparel'. In exchange, Robert Chantrell was to pay Soane one hundred guineas.[15] It was not unusual that Chantrell was

---

[13] George Basevi, one of Chantrell's fellow pupils, also had a father who was interested in the arts, had business interests on the Stock Exchange and 'knew Soane very well': A. T. Bolton, *Architectural Education a Century Ago* [n.d.], p.3. Charles Tyrrell, another fellow pupil, was the 'Son of Timothy Tyrrell, a solicitor who was an old friend of . . . Soane': Colvin, p.846. *The Westminster Review*, XLI (1844), p.73, in an article critical of the state of English Architecture, states '. . . the choice of the instructor in the art [of architecture] is entirely guided by family connexions or acquaintance . . .'.

[14] In the earlier and later parts of Soane's career he had smaller numbers of pupils. Chantrell was a pupil from June 1807 to January 1814. During this period his fellow pupils were: Charles Malton, Feb. 1802–Dec. 1809; James Adams, May 1806–June 1809; George Bailey, a pupil from Aug. 1806 who subsequently became an assistant and stayed in the office until Jan. 1837; John Buxton, Nov. 1809–May 1814; George Basevi, Dec. 1810–June 1816; Charles Tyrrell, Jan. 1811–March 1817; Edward Foxhall, Nov. 1812–Jan. 1821.

[15] SM, Private Correspondence, xv, 16.

fourteen when the articles came into effect,[16] but there are other aspects of the document which are curious. The premiums which Soane charged his pupils were not consistent, nor do they appear to have been related to the intended length of apprenticeship. One hundred and fifty guineas was the norm charged by Soane in the first two decades of the century; some pupils paid 125 or 175 guineas but not since 1792 was anyone recorded as having paid as little as Chantrell, with the exception of Brinsley John Storace who paid a nominal five shillings. It is possible that the premium was related to the depth of friendship which existed between Soane and the pupil's father or it could have been linked to Soane's perception of what the father could afford to pay. In most cases the indenture was signed after the pupil entered the office 'as there was usually a probationary period of some weeks or longer'.[17] However, in Chantrell's case he did not enter the office until 15 June 1807, five months after the signing of the articles. There is no apparent explanation for this delay which is unparalleled among Soane's other pupils.

In the early nineteenth century, the standard method of acquiring an architectural education was through an apprenticeship served in the office of an established architect. By this time most of the London designers took pupils and occasionally a provincial architect would do the same. However, the quality of training received varied considerably and the system was open to abuse; at its worst the pupil was exploited as a source of free labour.[18] On the other hand it enabled the pupil to gain valuable practical experience that would not have been available to a student attending a full-time course at

---

[16] Of his fellow pupils, Malton and Bailey also came at fourteen but Basevi and Tyrrell were both sixteen and Adams did not enter the office until he was twenty-one: Bolton, *Architectural Education*, p.3.

[17] A. T. Bolton, *The Works of Sir John Soane* (1924), p.xxxix.

[18] 'A young man designing to enter the profession is apprenticed for seven years to an architect, not on account of his eminence, for none of our great architects have a school of followers, nor do any of them take more pupils than are required to perform the drudgery of the office . . . This period of service is spent in copying papers or designs of the most commonplace buildings, and in working out the details of carpentry and bricklaying. It is not pretended that the pupil is sent there to be instructed in the history of his art, nor to be taught the art of designing buildings according to any fixed or received theory; and if during his apprenticeship he picks up any artistic notions on the subject, he must have more enthusiasm or better opportunities than fall to the lot of most men. Pupils are taken to assist the master in carrying out his own designs, and to acquire what knowledge might stick to them in so doing; whatever they learn beyond that is their own . . .': *Westminster Review*, XLI (1844), p.73, *et seq.*

an academy,[19] and some architects took seriously the responsibility for their pupils' education. Soane belonged to this category and the high regard in which he was held by at least some of his former pupils is a testimony to the benefits which they received from him.[20]

The period of Chantrell's pupilage saw Soane engaged on all of the buildings which are now considered to be his major artistic achievements: Chelsea Hospital (1809–17); the Picture Gallery and Mausoleum at Dulwich (1811–14); 13 Lincoln's Inn Fields (1812–13); the Bank of England (the commission ran throughout the period 1807–14). Chantrell could not have chosen a more auspicious time to be in Soane's office, but the education which his pupils received went far beyond engaging in menial tasks to assist the master with his projects. Indeed, relatively little of the pupils' time was spent on Soane's buildings; instead they studied a more comprehensive range of buildings which illustrated many of the important periods of architectural achievement.

Soane's life was almost totally dedicated to his profession and he demanded the same commitment from those who worked for him. In the first of his annual series of Royal Academy lectures he warned the students that 'from earliest youth not a moment must be lost by him who desires to become a great architect',[21] and the same words could well have guided his own pupils. Their indentures give the office hours as 7 am to 7 pm in the summer and 8 am to 8 pm in the winter, although throughout the year the pupils signed in in the 'Day Book' at a more reasonable time, usually between 9 am and 9.30 am. The Day Books also contain a record of the daily work of each pupil, and their survival enables an accurate picture to be assembled of Chantrell's programme of study.[22] The activities in which he engaged can, for convenience, be divided into seven categories: Classical orders and ornament; ancient Classical buildings; Italian, French and English Renaissance architecture; projects associated with Soane's own buildings; reduction of drawings for

---

[19] In this respect, English architectural education in the nineteenth century was seen as superior to the French system of full-time study at the Ecole des Beaux Arts.

[20] For instance, letters written in Rome by John Sanders to his former master Soane suggest a strong friendship existed between them: A. T. Bolton, *A Portrait of Sir John Soane* (1927) p.252, *et seq.* See also D. Stroud, *The Architecture of Sir John Soane* (1961), p.29.

[21] J. Soane, *Lectures in Architecture*, ed. A. T. Bolton (1929), p.16.

[22] A full list of Chantrell's activities while a pupil, taken from Soane's Day Books, appears in Webster, Appendix 1.

'The Book';[23] the production of lecture diagrams, used by Soane to illustrate his Royal Academy lectures;[24] and, finally, the computing of accounts, on which the staff worked spasmodically, and often together, presumably at various stages of individual contracts. Entries do not normally mention the building to which the accounts refer, except in the case of 'The Bank', the accounts for which consumed a vast amount of time.

Soane kept much of the work produced by his pupils. Although only rarely did they sign their drawings, there are a small number of them in the Soane Museum which can, with some certainty, be ascribed to Chantrell. They are all views or elevations of the work of others and thus it is not possible to come to any conclusion about the quality of Chantrell's own designs in this period. What they reveal about his skills as a draughtsman is not always impressive. On the whole, the standard of the elevations is better than that of the perspectives, and drawings on a small scale tend to be better than those on a large scale. Perhaps it was in an attempt to improve the quality of his drawings that Soane required Chantrell to spend almost the whole of his last year in the office drawing views of London buildings.

An analysis of Chantrell's course of study as set out in the Day Books reveals that it was essentially conservative and academic. It began with a study of the architectural orders and important Roman buildings, and subsequently examined the work of architects such as Palladio, Vignola, Jones, Wren, Burlington, Kent and Chambers. But, somewhat surprisingly, it proceeded no further along this chronological path. Given Soane's position as a neo-Classical architect of international importance, one might expect that, included in his pupil's studies, there would have been at least a representative selection of designs and philosophies of the recent more 'advanced' architects and theorists such as the Abbé Laugier[25]

---

[23] This Book, or, more correctly, Books, contained relatively small-scale versions of the finished drawings for the various building projects with which Soane was involved.

[24] Soane spent much of his 'spare time' in 1806–07 in the preparation of the texts for these, and in 1809 and 1810 the diagrams were produced. Although on occasions all the office staff was involved with these, it appears that Chantrell devoted more time to them than anyone else in the office.

[25] However, Soane is known to have owned 11 copies of his *Essai sur l'Architecture*. Furthermore, Bolton believes that Soane's own philosophy of architecture, as expounded in his Royal Academy lectures, was heavily dependent on Laugier, and suggests that Soane might have used the *Essai* as 'a gift book for pupils': Bolton, *Portrait*, pp. 142–43.

and C. N. Ledoux.[26] However, one week of 'drawing urns from Piranesi' is the only Day Book reference to Chantrell's contact with European neo-Classicism. There are numerous references to the pupils going out to sketch or measure architecture in London but, interestingly, at least from the evidence of the Day Books, Chantrell was not directed to the works of George Dance or Henry Holland, two of the most gifted and original English architects of the late eighteenth century, both of whom produced buildings which were accessible and are known to have been admired by Soane. Even more surprising is that relatively little time was spent in studying Soane's own buildings; clearly he did not attempt to impose his own somewhat idiosyncratic style on his pupils.

Complementing the study of architectural design was the development of a number of more practical skills. In particular, time spent on the accounts, which would have involved estimating and checking bills of quantity, would have been useful experience for a prospective architect. On occasions two or three of the pupils would go out to measure, and produce, a plan of a specific building. On 16 August 1811 Chantrell produced from his own measurements a plan of a house in Fleet Street, and he spent 16 and 17 July 1813 in 'taking a plan, elevation and section of Dr Bell's House, Westminster'. However, such activities are confined to occasional days, fitted in between weeks of drawing exercises. It is recorded that another pupil, George Basevi, 'had a day's work with the head of the office measuring mason's work',[27] but there are no similar entries made by Chantrell. It is apparent that during the years of pupilage, only a very limited time – possibly none at all – was devoted specifically to building construction and the routine management of a building project. The most likely form of exposure to these aspects of professional activity would have been through a practical involvement in the commissions on which Soane was engaged, but this seems to have been the task of the office assistants rather than the pupils. Certainly Chantrell spent time working on drawings of Soane's buildings – although this occupied less time than many of the other areas listed above – but it is important that a distinction is made here between theoretical and practical studies. The principal means by which Chantrell came into contact with Soane's work was through the production of drawings for the Book. In fact only

[26] C. N. Ledoux *L'Architecture considerée sous le rapport de l'art* . . . had been published in 1804, and between 1807 and 1814 its contents would surely have been seen as topical.
[27] Bolton, *Architectural Education*, p. 3.

rarely did Chantrell have direct experience of Soane's projects in the sense that he was engaged in tasks which would have been of any real use to Soane in the execution of any scheme and thus enable Chantrell to further his understanding of an architect's responsibilities. Moreover, where such cases do arise, the project was often worked on by several members of the staff together. Since it was normal for them to work independently, it is possible that it was only when drawings were needed urgently by Soane that the pupils were diverted from their theoretical studies. During the last three years of his indentures when, presumably, he would have been of most use to Soane, Chantrell spent a total of only about fifteen weeks on activities associated with Soane's buildings, and the last year was taken up entirely with theoretical studies and drawings of the work of others. The entries in the Day Books do not specify that the pupils spent the entire working day in the office, but neither is there a single entry that states unambiguously that Chantrell ever accompanied Soane to see work in progress. A. T. Bolton was of the opinion that 'pupils . . . visited works in hand, in pairs and had to take sketches . . . they must in this way have acquired an excellent idea of the construction actually in execution'.[28] However, it seems, as far as one can deduce from the Day Book entries for Chantrell, that the practicalities of building construction and site management were given scant coverage.

Despite their completeness, the Day Books give only a factual outline of what was studied, valuable though that is. What they do not reveal is the philosophy which underpinned the pupils' studies. However, at the same time that Chantrell was in Soane's office the master was preparing and then perfecting his course of Royal Academy professorial lectures, which it is reasonable to assume can be taken as a more precise source of information for Soane's philosophy of architectural education. Whereas, the Day Books suggest a syllabus dominated by copying drawings of important buildings, in the first of his lectures Soane urged his audience not to copy but to be '. . . intimately acquainted with not only what the ancients have done, but endeavour to learn from their Works what they would have done. We shall thereby become Artists and not mere Copyists; . . .'.[29] In Lecture XI he stated 'Imitation of masters is not required in Architects . . . it may make them humble mannerists, but this method of study will never make a great artist'.[30]

[28] *Ibid.*
[29] Soane, *Lectures*, p. 16.
[30] *Ibid.*, p. 172

But how were Soane's pupils to develop these skills of originality? Chantrell, like many of his fellow pupils submitted drawings of original compositions to the annual Royal Academy exhibitions,[31] yet the time spent on their production is not recorded in the Day Books. It is possible of course that the students were expected to devote a significant amount of their leisure time to the production of original designs based on examples studied in office hours, and in this way become 'artists' and develop the skills needed in architectural composition. In this respect it is, perhaps, of significance that Chantrell's Royal Academy entries are recorded as having been sent from his home address, rather than from Soane's office.[32]

In the context of Chantrell's subsequent career it is interesting to consider how far his training equipped him for the professional path which he was to follow.[33] In particular, did the historical content of his training reflect Soane's lack of philosophical sympathy with Gothic? It appears that in the carefully arranged survey of historical architecture which Soane's pupils followed, the middle ages were completely ignored. The only specific references to Gothic architecture appear in 1807, when he spent a week 'about Ramsay Abbey', a house which Soane had Gothicised in 1804, and, on 6 February 1813, the entire office staff spent the day on drawings of Stockport church which had been rebuilt in the Gothic style in 1813–17, to the designs of Lewis Wyatt. It is possible that these represent Chantrell's only official contact with the style during his seven year training. Soane's Royal Academy lectures in fact reveal a good deal about his attitude to Gothic: while he acknowledged that some cathedrals were 'truly sublime', the style was not afforded any of the detailed analysis devoted to Classicism. He urged students to study Gothic 'not for its taste but for its effect in mass and detail'.[34] He made no attempt to explain Gothic principles of composition – something that subsequently Chantrell spent years trying to understand, as he admitted later;[35] nor did Soane acknowledge the period's sophisticated structural solutions.

---

[31] The Exhibition *Catalogue* records that he exhibited the following: in 1812, Design for a Cenotaph, no. 857 (p.37); in 1813, Design for a church, no. 834 (p.35) and Design for a public library, no. 887 (p.37).

[32] *Ibid.*, 1812, p.44; 1813, p.45.

[33] This issue is examined in more detail in C. Webster, 'The Influence of Sir John Soane', in *Late Georgian Classicism*, eds. Roger White and Caroline Lightburn (1988), pp.28–31.

[34] J. Soane, *Lectures*, p.82.

[35] *Builder*, V (1847), p.300.

PLATE I (a)   LEEDS: PUBLIC BATHS, 1819–21.

PLATE I (b)   LEEDS: PHILOSOPHICAL AND LITERARY SOCIETY HALL, 1819–20.
Watercolour, perhaps by Chantrell.

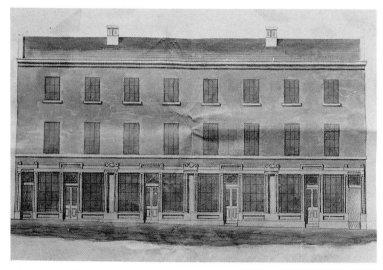

PLATE 2 (a)   LEEDS: SHOPS IN BOND STREET, DESIGNED FOR WILLIAM HEY, 1820.
Drawing by Chantrell.

PLATE 2 (b)   LEEDS: SHOPS IN BOND STREET, DESIGNED FOR WILLIAM HEY, 1820.
Alternative design. Drawing by Chantrell.

PLATE 3 (a)   LEEDS: CHRIST CHURCH, SCHOOL, 1841–42.

PLATE 3 (b)   LEEDS: ST MARY, QUARRY HILL, SCHOOL, 1829
Chantrell's design was for a single storey building. Alterations, including the addition
of the upper floor, were undertaken by C. W. Burleigh in 1848.

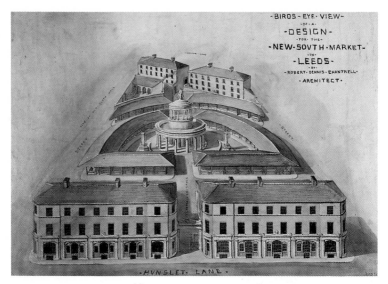

PLATE 4 (a)   LEEDS: SOUTH MARKET, 1823–24.
Drawing by Chantrell.

PLATE 4 (b)   LEEDS: SOUTH MARKET, 1823–24, INITIAL DESIGN FOR THE CROSS.
Drawing by Chantrell, c.1823.

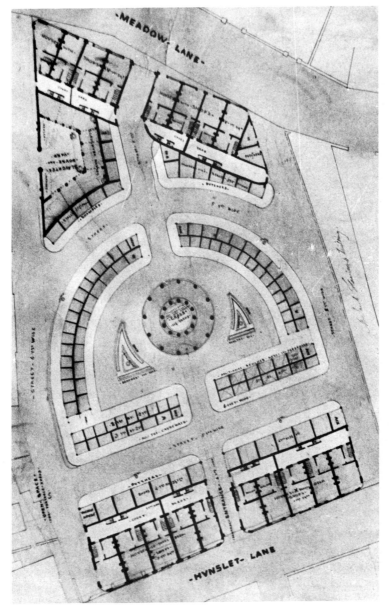

PLATE 5   LEEDS: SOUTH MARKET, 1823–24, PLAN.
Drawing by Chantrell.

PLATE 6 (a)   BRUGES: FISH MARKET, 1821, ARCHITECT UNKNOWN.
From an early nineteenth century engraving.

PLATE 6 (b)   HUNSLET, LEEDS: ST MARY
Watercolour by N. R. Rhodes showing the tower which Chantrell added to the
eighteenth century chapel in 1830.

PLATE 7 (a)   LEEDS: COURT HOUSE, DESIGNED BY THOMAS TAYLOR, 1811.
Engraving by Whittock and Sims, 1829.

PLATE 7 (b)   LEEDS: COURT HOUSE.
Late nineteenth century photograph showing Chantrell's alterations of 1827–34.

PLATE 8 (a)   LEEDS: GATELODGE, INTENDED TO BE BUILT 'ON THE ESTATE OF THE LATE
JOHN ATKINSON ESQ'S TRUSTEES'.
Watercolour by Chantrell.

PLATE 8 (b)   ARMITAGE BRIDGE, NEAR HUDDERSFIELD: ARMITAGE BRIDGE HOUSE,
ENTRANCE FRONT.

Similarly, the Tudor style, which Chantrell adopted on several occasions towards the end of his career, found little favour with Soane: in Lecture V he accused it of exhibiting 'the most extraordinary absurdities', and complained that 'this licentious, whimsical and capricious mode continued unrestrained by scientific laws and unfettered by Reason . . .'.[36]

The Royal Academy lectures contain a significant emphasis on the development of skills other than those which are basically artistic and compositional. Early in the course, students were told that they '. . . must be conversant in Arithmatic, Geometry, Mechanics and Hydraulics . . . [and] the theory and practice of Perspective . . . [They must be able to] draw the human figure with taste and correctness, and have a complete knowledge of Painting and Sculpture . . .'.[37] In later lectures Soane stresses the need for sound foundations in buildings and explains ways of preventing fires and outbreaks of dry-rot.[38] It is therefore rather surprising to discover that none of these subjects, with the exception of perspective, appears to have been dealt with in the office, at least according to the Day Books. It is of course possible that Soane considered that his duty to his pupils was to supply only a theoretical education and that this academic course would at some point be supplemented by additional study. Perhaps one can interpret Soane's concept of architectural education as ideally having three components: articled pupilage; foreign travel; practical experience of building construction. There are numerous references to the importance which Soane attached to foreign travel;[39] those intending to enter the profession should 'complete [their] studies with a period of study abroad',[40] he told his audience in Lecture XII. Such a course was taken by George Basevi; soon after the completion of his pupilage with Soane, in 1816, he set out for Italy and Greece. Although Soane is less explicit about the value of experience of building sites, it is clear that he saw it as essential.[41] This could, of course, be gained during pupilage but often it was experienced separately, while working with a

---

[36] J. Soane, *Lectures*, p.88.

[37] *Ibid.*, p.15.

[38] *Ibid.*, p.189.

[39] In his memoirs he recorded that his own winning of a travelling scholarship was the 'most fortunate event of my life . . . [for] it was the means by which I formed those connections to which I owe all the advantages I have since enjoyed . . .', quoted in Stroud, p.22.

[40] J. Soane, *Lectures*, p.192.

[41] Soane's apparent avoidance of stating clearly that prospective architects should spend some time working for a builder could be explained in terms of his objections, on ethical grounds, to architects acting as builders, and vice versa.

tradesman or surveyor; Soane was himself the son of a bricklayer, several of his pupils were sons of builders or surveyors, and early nineteenth-century architects such as Thomas Taylor and Charles Barry are known to have spent time working for builders. If Soane expected his pupils either to have had site experience already or to acquire it subsequently, that would adequately explain its apparent omission from the pupils' syllabus. But, however it was gained, the importance which Soane attached to it is clear; in Lecture XII he expounds the importance of a 'thorough knowledge of Construction, and of the Nature and Quality of [building materials] . . . Nothing is so well calculated to insure the Architects' success in life, as without this knowledge, which can only be obtained by great experience and attentive observation, formed on real practice, all his other attainments will be of little avail'.[42]

Chantrell's last appearance in Soane's office was on 31 January 1814, seven years and two weeks after his articles had been signed, and the week after his twenty-first birthday. For him then to have embarked on foreign travel would have been extremely difficult as the Napoleonic Wars rendered most of Europe closed to Englishmen at this time. Anyway, Chantrell appears to have had interests in another direction; on 12 February 1814 he married Elizabeth Caroline Boham at St Mary Magdalene, Bermondsey.[43] The first publication of the banns was the day before his birthday, and it would seem clear that the ceremony was arranged to take place as soon after his attainment of majority and freedom from indentures as was possible.

There is evidence to suggest that soon after leaving Soane's office, Chantrell had set himself up as an architect, perhaps working from his home in south London. He appears in Underhill's *Triennial Directory of London, Westminster and Southwark* where he is listed under 'Architects' and 'Nobility and Gentry' in the edition for the years 1817, 1818 and 1819, which probably was published in 1816. Both entries give his address as 6 Crown Row, Walworth. However it is likely that his attempts to establish an architectural career started rather earlier, but the previous edition of Underhill's *Directory*, for the years 1814, 1815 and 1816 would have been compiled just before he parted from Soane.[44] In the Royal Academy's summer exhibition

[42] J. Soane, *Lectures*, p. 182.

[43] GLRO, Bermondsey Parish Records: St Mary Magdalene, Register of Marriages, (1813–22). The marriage was witnessed by John Wheeler (who appears frequently in the register as a witness and was probably a verger or pew opener), Mary Caxhead and Sarah Boddy.

[44] Underhill's is the only directory of this period to give a thorough coverage of the Walworth area.

of 1814 Chantrell displayed a 'View of a design for a series of dwelling houses, intended to form one side of a square',[45] no doubt hoping that it would bring him to the attention of potential patrons. When his first child, also called Robert Dennis, was baptised in February 1815, Chantrell referred to himself as 'architect' in the register,[46] and later that year it is likely that he submitted a design for the new London Institution building. This was subsequently erected to the design of William Brooks, and the Institute's records[47] contain no mention of which other architects sent in schemes. However, in 1823 Chantrell exhibited at the Northern Society for the Encouragement of the Arts a 'View of an edifice designed for the London Institute for Literature and Philosophy'[48] which was almost certainly one of the rejected designs.[49]

Whether Chantrell secured any architectural commissions at this time is questionable, but it is clear that he could hardly have chosen a less auspicious time to launch his career. As Sir John Summerson has pointed out, the war with France had almost halted building in London[50] and there were already a number of highly talented architects who could find little or no employment in this period.[51] Furthermore, since Chantrell's 'office' was actually in a village on the outskirts of London, his chances of attracting commissions were further reduced.[52]

---

[45] *The Exhibition of the Royal Academy, 1814*, p. 32, exhibit no. 706. Graves incorrectly records this item as a 'Design for a Villa' by Chantrell.

[46] GLRO, P92 MRY/22: Newington Parish Registers, p. 173.

[47] These are now in the Guildhall Library, London.

[48] Northern Society for the Encouragement of the Arts, *Catalogue*, exhibit no. 1.

[49] On 6 April 1815 the Proprietors of the Institute resolved that the Board of Managers should be empowered to 'receive plans and estimates for the building from different artists': Guildhall Library, London, MS. 2757 unfoliated. It is thus likely that Chantrell's design belongs to April 1815, or soon after, although Brooks was not appointed architect for the building until 22 January 1816: Guildhall Library, MS. 2751, p. 113. The building was usually referred to merely as the 'London Institution', but it appeared in S. Lewis, *Topographical Dictionary* (1835), under the heading 'Literary and Philosophical Institutions'. Chantrell no doubt used the extended name so that connections between this scheme, and the hall he had recently built for the Leeds Philosophical and Literary Society would not be lost on the visitors to the Northern Society's exhibition.

[50] J. Summerson, *Georgian London* (1969), pp. 154–62. He notes that state expenditure on buildings was withdrawn and an acute shortage of Baltic timber combined with high taxation on building materials discouraged individuals from embarking on building projects.

[51] *Ibid.*, p. 155. He includes Gandy, Tatham, Bond and Sanders in this category.

[52] Newington already had an established surveyor, Francis Hurlbatt (c. 1754–1834, see H. Colvin, *A Biographical Dictionary of British Architects, 1660–1840* (1978), p. 440). He is known to have been the author of some executed designs and probably supplied most of the modest demand for architectural services in the parish.

The extent and form of Chantrell's employment at this time must remain a matter for speculation, but given the affluence of his family he could have lived on an allowance from his father, and it need not be assumed he necessarily had any form of earned income. However, one possibility is worth examining; in the years around 1815 might Chantrell have worked for a builder or surveyor? It has been pointed out earlier that Soane stressed the importance of a prospective architect acquiring knowledge of good building practice, yet appears to have included little of this in the syllabus which the pupils followed. Since it is unlikely that Chantrell had worked on a site before entering Soane's office, this would have been the ideal time to gain such experience. This suggestion is not pure speculation for, when his second son was baptised in March 1816, he described himself as 'surveyor',[53] and not 'architect' as he had done at his first child's baptism the previous year. It is true that to a considerable extent, and certainly to the layman, the terms were interchangeable at this time, but it seems unlikely that anyone brought up with Soane's definite ideas about the importance of 'professionalism' would have been unaware of the significant distinction of quality implied by these terms.[54] There are numerous examples in this period of surveyors optimistically elevating themselves to the status of architect, but one would not expect someone like Chantrell to do the reverse without good reason. A point that stands out when one is considering Chantrell's subsequent commissions is that his buildings appear to have had a degree of durability that was by no means commonplace at the time, and Chantrell himself seems to have been especially skilled at handling complex structural problems. It appears probable, therefore, that the modest experience in these matters which he acquired in Soane's office had been substantially supplemented at some time before he arrived in Leeds in 1819.

The circumstances which led to Chantrell's professional appointment in Halifax are unknown, but he wrote in the *Builder* that 'In the year 1818 [I restored] the parapet and pinnacles of the parish church of Halifax'.[55] Moreover, in connection with the competition for the proposed Public Baths in Leeds, Chantrell wrote to the Baths secretary on 20 January 1819 and (probably) in February 1819,

[53] Newington Parish Registers, p.270.
[54] J. M. Crook, 'The pre-Victorian architect: professionalism and patronage', *Architectural History*, 12 (1969), pp.62–78. Crook points out that as early as 1773, an anonymous writer, possibly George Dance, judged any distinction between the two terms to be one of competence. By the 1830s the architect had established a more prestigious position for himself than the builder, engineer or surveyor.
[55] *Builder*, V (1847), p.300.

giving his address as 'Blackwall, Halifax'.[56] Most interestingly, in 1821 Chantrell wrote to Soane seeking advice on the designing of churches for the Commissioners, but goes on to say: 'my success in [securing the Leeds Baths commission has] caused my removal from Halifax where, since I had the pleasure of waiting upon you, I have resided as assistant to an architect, whose principles and ideas differed so widely from mine that I found I could never expect to reap any benefit from the connection . . .'.[57] So far as the chronology is concerned, the wording is ambiguous; 'since I had the pleasure of waiting on you' suggests that Chantrell had moved to Halifax soon after January 1814 (when his indentures expired) yet there is plenty of evidence, quoted already, to suggest that he was living in London until, at least, the spring of 1816. In the absence of further information, the issue of the date of his arrival in Halifax must remain open.

Who was the architect whom Chantrell assisted but with whom clearly he had no sympathy? There were only two architects in Halifax at this time, William Bradley and John Oates. Since Chantrell would have been working as an assistant when he 'restored the parapet and pinnacles of the parish church' one would expect his principal to be named in the church accounts and during 1818 they record various payments to Bradley for repairs to the church.[58] They make no mention of any payment to Oates. This would suggest fairly conclusively that it was with Bradley that Chantrell worked, and it is virtually confirmed by Miss Anne Lister of Shibden Hall who said of Bradley that he was 'not a man to be depended on – very idle – never right in his estimates – not fit to be an architect . . .'.[59] Whatever Bradley's shortcomings, it is most unlikely that Chantrell's time in Halifax was wasted. It was probably with him that Chantrell received his first professional employment, and had his first real contact with the far-from-genteel world of the building tradesmen. Certainly it would have represented his first contact with building practices in Yorkshire; no matter what experience he had gained in London there were still significant regional variations in such things as materials and constructional details that he would need to understand before embarking on an independent career in the county. His subsequent success in Leeds probably owed a good deal to what he learned in Halifax.

---

[56] LCA, DB 276: Leeds Public Baths, Committee Minute Book, 1818–27.
[57] SM, Private Correspondence, xv, A, 32. The letter is dated 6 Jan. 1821.
[58] WYJAS, Wakefield Office: Halifax Parish Church Account Book, 1760–1832.
[59] Quoted in Linstrum, p.35.

CHAPTER 3

Chantrell's Career in Leeds, 1819–1846

Chantrell's apprenticeship with Soane made him fully conversant with the practice and theory of Classicism, and with the more general issues of professional practice. But Soane represents the end of an era in the practice of architecture, an era in which architects for the most part designed country homes or public buildings in the Classical tradition, and were patronised by the world of discriminating, upper-class society. Conversely, Chantrell's career marks the beginning of a new era of crucial importance for the establishment of the professional practice of architecture in the provinces; an era in which an ambitious architect would have to design buildings of various types and various styles, sometimes using new materials, and work in a much more competitive environment for individual patrons and committees whose knowledge and taste in architecture could not always be taken for granted.[1] Perhaps the most remarkable aspect of Chantrell's career is the way in which he adapted to a rapidly changing situation in which the architects of his generation were required to work. In assessing the more tangible benefits which Chantrell received from Soane, although it is clear that he gained little to help him with the designing of Gothic churches,[2] one might expect to find that he was better prepared for the various secular commissions he obtained. However, even these presented problems of style or function for which his studies with Soane would not necessarily have equipped him to deal. Nevertheless, it is reasonable to conclude that, at the outset of his career in Leeds, Chantrell saw his own practice as following the model of Soane's and it was commissions for public buildings and houses which he pursued most actively.

[1] See: J. M. Crook, 'The Pre-Victorian Architect: Professionalism and Patronage', *Architectural History*, 12 (1969), pp.62–78, and J. Wilton-Ely, 'The Rise of the Professional Architect in England' in S. Kostof (ed.), *The Architect* (1977).
[2] See below, p.82. The designs adopted for Chantrell's ecclesiastical commissions are described and discussed in Chapter 4.

Chantrell was appointed as architect for the Public Baths, Leeds, on 4 March 1819,[3] eleven days before he left Halifax,[4] but the decision to move to Leeds pre-dated this appointment and can have been made only in the belief that the town offered promising prospects for an ambitious architect. His optimism proved to be well founded and, two months after securing the Baths commission, he was appointed architect of the new hall for the Philosophical and Literary Society in Leeds.[5] These two commissions were responsible for establishing Chantrell's reputation. They were the town's first important public buildings since the Court House of 1811–13 (Plate 7(a)), and even before the buildings were close to completion they aroused public interest. The years around 1820 were a period of relative optimism and prosperity, and Leeds, like the other British towns and cities, became increasingly conscious of the need for 'improvement', following the lead set by London and Edinburgh. Chantrell's London training, and first-hand experience of the latest developments there, must have made him appear especially attractive to potential employers at this time. He was not unique in respect of his experience but the only other professionally trained architect in the town, Thomas Taylor, was devoting the bulk of his time to ecclesiastical commissions over a wide geographical area, leaving, as the only competition for Chantrell in Leeds, a handful of men

[3] LCA, DB 276: Leeds Public Baths, Committee Minute Book, 1818–27.
[4] Chantrell's arrival in Leeds can be dated with some degree of certainty to 15 March 1819: the letter which accompanied the plans he submitted for the Public Baths, Leeds, gave his address as 'Saddle Yard, Briggate, or Blackwall, Halifax till 15 March': Miscellaneous letters in the Public Baths papers, LCA, DB 276. This letter can be dated to the period between 24 Jan. 1819, when he wrote to request particulars, and 18 Feb. 1819, when a meeting of the building committee was held which noted the submission of his plans. One might assume from this that Chantrell was in Halifax on a temporary basis and that he had settled in Leeds earlier, but this would seem to be incorrect; in a letter to Soane, dated 6 Jan. 1821, Chantrell wrote '. . . during a residence in Leeds of 20 months . . .': SM, Private Correspondence, xv, A, 32. Chantrell's father wrote to Soane on 16 May 1820 '. . . my son . . . settled last year in his profession of an architect at Leeds . . .': SM, Private Correspondence, xv, A, 32. However, the issue of the date on which Chantrell arrived in Leeds is not totally resolved. For four weeks from 10 Aug. 1818 there appeared in the *Leeds Intelligencer* an advertisement offering rooms to let in the Saddle Yard, but no similar advertisement appeared between Sept. 1818 and March 1819. Furthermore, an advertisement was published in the edition of 27 July 1818 requiring a 'large commodious room to rent . . . as near to Briggate as possible . . . with good lights', but the advertiser's name is not given.
[5] *LI*, 3 May 1819, announced that the meeting to select the architect for the hall would take place on 7 May 1819, but the Building Committee Book suggests that it was on 14 May 1819 that the appointment was made: LUL, Philosophical and Literary Society Papers, No. 6, Building Committee Book.

who called themselves 'architects' but almost certainly had neither the knowledge nor the inclination to conduct their businesses in a totally professional manner.

Chantrell's success in securing the appointment to design the new premises for the Leeds Public Baths Company was impressive; his was one of fifteen entries and his competitors included Thomas Rickman of Liverpool and Decimus Burton from London.[6] The finished building consisted of 'two separate and complete suites of apartments . . . for ladies and gentlemen',[7] and it was described as 'a highly elegant and classical, though diminutive building . . . The entrance is marked by two couples of Ionic columns supporting an entablature, and a richly chiselled panel, where, among the foliage is seen the esculapian serpent: at the end of the building are coupled pilasters'.[8] The only known illustration of the now demolished building is a crude engraving which appeared in the *Baths Company Handbook*, *c*.1838 (Plate 1(a)).[9] Suites of public baths in the form of a small, but architecturally imposing, single storied building, can be traced back to the eighteenth century, and especially to Bath.[10] But whereas the baths of that city use a variety of architectural idioms including Baroque and Adamesque neo-Classicism, Chantrell used an adaptation of Soane's style. It would appear from the engraving of the Baths' facade that there was a stele head containing an anthemion over each column and pilaster, and in the centre, above the entablature, was a panel of incised, perhaps 'Greek Key', decoration. Taken as a whole, the facade is in fact a scaled-down and simplified version of the east end of Soane's Lothbury facade of the Bank of England of 1795.

On 14 May 1819, Chantrell's design was selected for the Philosophical and Literary Hall in Leeds (Plate 1(b)). This was about ten weeks after his appointment to build the Public Baths, and the construction of these two buildings progressed almost simultaneously during the following two years. The Hall contained a lecture room in the form of an amphitheatre, a library, a laboratory and galleries for the display of items of natural history. In plan, the

---

[6] Leeds Public Baths, Committee Minute Book, 1818–27.

[7] E. Baines, *History, Directory and Gazetteer of the County of York*, 2 vols (Leeds, 1822), I, p.22.

[8] J. Heaton (publisher), *Walk Through Leeds* (Leeds [*c*.1835]), p.7.

[9] There is a copy in the LCA, DB 276.

[10] At about the same time that the Leeds Baths were being built, buildings of a similar type were being erected at Scarborough, Lockwood (near Huddersfield) and elsewhere. Certainly it was an increasingly common building type but there is no evidence that Chantrell built any baths other than those in Leeds.

building was rectangular and its two principal facades were adjacent to each other, facing Park Row and Bond Street. It was of two stories, the lower one rusticated and the upper adorned by Doric pilasters, either in pairs or as singles. Descriptions of the building in the first half of the nineteenth century usually applied the word 'handsome', whereas in the same publications the Baths were described as 'elegant'. The distinction is an appropriate one. The hall of a society established to encourage cultural pursuits would not have been considered the place for the 'fashionable' motifs used at the baths.[11] Instead, Chantrell produced a dignified and conservative design whose only concession to the style of Soane and the Greek Revivalists is the panelled blocks placed above the cornice. However, these, devoid of Greek scrolls, statues or stele heads, lose much of their modernity. The building belongs to the late-Georgian local tradition of modest-sized Classical public buildings.

The two commissions had an added importance at this early stage in Chantrell's career; the finished buildings were used almost exclusively by the principal inhabitants of the town, the very people whose support he needed in order to establish a thriving architectural practice. Not only was he thus able to display his professional skills in the design and erection of the buildings but, on a more personal level, his meetings with the respective building committees would have enabled him to demonstrate that he held values similar to their own. They would have found that their architect was a supporter of the Church of England, the Conservative party and the 'provincial enlightenment'.

The beneficial connections which Chantrell made through these early commissions are illustrated by his work for William Hey and Benjamin Gott. Hey was present at the initial meeting called to discuss the erection of the Public Baths, and he had been on the council of the Philosophical and Literary Society from its inception. In 1820 he commissioned Chantrell to design a block of four shops in Bond Street, Leeds.[12] The shops were to be of three stories, the upper two being quite plain, but, on the ground floor, the doors and large windows of the shops were surrounded with the latest 'Grecian' ornament (Plates 2(a) and (b)). This was derived in part from aspects of Soane's Bank of England, especially the decoration

[11] In 1825, Chantrell's unexecuted design for the Commercial Buildings in Leeds was criticised for using 'too florid an order of architecture': *LI*, 7 July 1825.

[12] Nos 4, 5, 6 and 7, Bond Street. Two alternative designs were submitted and are dated 20 April 1820 (LCA, DB 75/9: Hey Estate).

of the Tivoli Corner, and Chantrell's designs, in general terms, reflected the contemporary belief that the designers of shop fronts need not be concerned with architectural propriety; visual impact was more important than archaeological scholarship.[13] The design of the shops shows that the restraint of the Philosophical and Literary Hall was not the result of any inability on Chantrell's behalf to design in a more fashionable idiom. Benjamin Gott, for whom, between 1823 and 1847, Chantrell designed various buildings at Armley and Leeds,[14] was a member of the building committee of the Public Baths and also of the council of the Philosophical and Literary Society from its inception. The relationship between Gott and Chantrell certainly went beyond the formal meetings of the architect and his building committee, and as early as 1820 the two men were on sufficiently good terms for Gott to introduce Chantrell to Sir James Graham. Soon after, Chantrell 'designed a small church intended to be erected on [Graham's] property . . .',[15] although it seems that it was never built. There is no reason for thinking that Chantrell did not form equally important professional or social relationships with other members of these building committees.

During 1821 Chantrell was involved with three commissions which, although neither as prestigious nor as lucrative as his first two appointments, nevertheless demonstrated his professional talents to the more prosperous and influential sections of the community. These were for the modernisation and improvement of two important public buildings in Leeds, the Music Hall and the Library, and a design for the proposed Baths for the Poor in Harrogate. The design for the latter was approved but execution had to be abandoned through lack of finance. The Baths Charity was actively supported by the Earl of Harewood and it was he who presided at the meeting which accepted Chantrell's scheme.[16]

In 1821 Chantrell began work on two ecclesiastical commissions: the old chapel at Bramley and Christ Church, Leeds. At Bramley

---

[13] See D. Dean, *English Shop Fronts, 1792–1840* (1970), which reproduces plates from I. and J. Taylor, *Designs for Shop Fronts* (1792), and J. Young, *A Series of Designs for Shop Fronts* (1828). The shops which formed the front of Francis Goodwin's Central Market, Leeds, 1824–27, illustrated in Linstrum, p. 316, had decoration similar to that found in the Chantrell designs.

[14] From 1823 to 1844 Chantrell supervised various alterations and extensions to the chapel at Armley, paid for by Gott. Chantrell was probably the designer of the school and almshouses at Armley which Gott had built in 1832, and in 1845–47 Chantrell built St Philip's, Leeds, where Gott's business was the principal benefactor.

[15] SM, Private Correspondence, xv, A, 32: Chantrell to Soane, 6 Jan. 1821.

[16] *LI*, 3 Sept. 1821.

he merely added a small bell turret to the existing structure but the successful completion of Christ Church (Plate 11(b)) was to become one of the most important buildings of his career in that it introduced him to the commissioners who administered the Church Building Acts, and led to his eventual specialisation in ecclesiastical commissions. However, it is doubtful whether Chantrell could have foreseen its significance at this time.

Unlike the members of the building committees for the Baths and Philosophical Hall, the chapelwardens at Bramley were neither influential nor likely to have been especially discriminating. Nevertheless, after Chantrell had erected their new bell turret they must have joined the growing ranks of his satisfied patrons for in 1822 he was asked to produce plans and estimates for a proposed extension and replacement of the chapel (Plate 11(a)).[17] In 1823 he designed and built a new vicarage in Bramley, in 1824 and 1828 he produced further proposals for new churches for the village, and in 1833 he substantially extended the old chapel. This is only one of numerous instances where a single patron or committee engaged Chantrell for several separate commissions spread over a number of years. He seems to have been skilled at dealing with his clients and, in most instances, they were pleased with what he produced for them. His fee for the 1821 bell turret cannot have been more than a few pounds, yet the commissions to which it subsequently led illustrated the importance of accepting any appointment, no matter how modest. No doubt it was a principle Chantrell followed and throughout his career apparently minor commissions run concurrently with his more important ones. For instance, in 1824 he superintended the rebuilding of the boundary wall around the Free School, Leeds, the entire cost of the work being £34 18s., and in 1825 he received £12 12s. 0d. for supervising various minor repairs to the Free School.

From the early 1820s Chantrell was accepting commissions in which his artistic, as opposed to architectural, skills could be exercised. On a number of occasions he produced small-scale perspective views to illustrate maps or layouts for the Leeds surveyor Charles Fowler. For example, his illustration of the Toll Houses at Barnsdale, near Doncaster, appears in Fowler's 'Plan of Several Turnpike Roads between Leeds and Doncaster', published in 1822, and included in Fowler's 'Plan of the Leeds Race Ground' of 1823 is

[17] ICBS, 413 (Bramley): neither of these schemes was carried out.

a view of the Grandstand, engraved after a drawing by Chantrell.[18] The artistic commissions he undertook suggest two things: that it was necessary for him to supplement his income from the practice of architecture, and that he saw these as an additional source of useful publicity, and as a basis for potentially more important collaborations with Fowler.

In yet more ways, Chantrell sought to advertise his skills discreetly. In September 1822 he exhibited at the Yorkshire Horticultural Society 'a design and elevation for a residence, and plan of four acres of garden and pleasure grounds' which was 'much admired'.[19] There is no other known instance of an artist or architect displaying such schemes before the Society at this time. The Northern Society for the Encouragement of the Arts was revived in 1822,[20] and in that year it held an exhibition after a lapse of eleven years. The venue for this was the picture gallery of the Music Hall, Leeds, which Chantrell had transformed the year before by adding top lighting. Together with Anthony Salvin, Thomas Taylor and others, he exhibited 'several clever architectural designs and views',[21] in the architecture section.[22] Subsequently, he exhibited with the Society in 1823, 1825 and 1830, all the occasions on which modern architectural drawings were accepted for display. Important as all these activities were in helping to establish his career, the most valuable and consistent publicity came through the pages of the *Leeds Intelligencer*. Why this should have been so is not clear, yet the support it gave him cannot be explained simply as representing the paper's objective assessment of contemporary architecture in Leeds. Indeed, while the paper was concerned with new buildings in so far as they were tangible signs of the status and prosperity of the town, it rarely made qualitative judgements about these structures and often omitted the name of the architect responsible. In contrast, almost every one of Chantrell's building projects was noted and

---

[18] The inscription under the illustration is 'R. D. Chantrell, Architectus, Leeds . . . Delin'. The inclusion of 'Delin' would suggest Chantrell merely drew the buildings rather than that he designed them but since the Toll Houses and Grandstand were recent buildings at the time they were drawn, it is not inconceivable that Chantrell was the architect of these schemes.

[19] *LI*, 9 Sept. 1822.

[20] T. Fawcett, *The Rise of English Provincial Art* (1974).

[21] *LI*, 27 May 1822. Taylor's contribution included a 'correct and spirited representation' of the interior of York Minster.

[22] See W. H. Thorp, *John N. Rhodes* (Leeds, 1901), p. 14. '. . . foremost among the local men who were practising [architecture] in Leeds and the surrounding county and exhibited designs for churches and other buildings of importance was R. D. Chantrell'.

was usually accompanied by enthusiastic approval. Towards the end of his residence in Leeds he himself often wrote the accounts of his buildings which appeared in the paper and it seems likely that earlier descriptions are, at least in part, also by him, although this was not acknowledged. Even after he had left Leeds, his activities were reported on a number of occasions. Some examples will usefully amplify these observations about Chantrell and the *Intelligencer*. On 20 October 1838 it reported that a new organ screen had been erected at St Mark's, Leeds, hardly a matter of importance outside the parish, and added 'the honour of the design belongs to Mr Chantrell'. Two weeks later the paper discussed the opening of St George's, Leeds. This was a building of major significance in the town as it was the first new church in Leeds for over ten years and was the town's first instance in that century of a new church financed entirely by public subscription. The design of St George's received no words of praise nor was its architect, John Clark, mentioned. The school attached to Christ Church, Leeds (Plate 3(a)), which Chantrell built in 1841–42, was a structure which, at best, could only be described as functional or unobtrusive; the opinion that it was ugly would not be difficult to sustain. As it 'approached completion' the expectation that it would be a 'spacious and elegant structure' was recorded,[23] and its completion was greeted enthusiastically.[24] Chantrell kept the editor informed about his commissions and the latter saw to it that these were published in a form that was invaluable to Chantrell. There must be an explanation for this but, so far, it remains hidden.

As a result of hard work, useful publicity, and the absence of serious competition, it took Chantrell only a few years to establish himself as the town's leading architect.[25] His enhanced status is reflected in his change of address. His first office had been in the Saddle Yard, Briggate,[26] one of the less desirable parts of the town,

---

[23] *LI*, 15 Jan. 1841.

[24] *Ibid.*, 2 April 1842: 'It is simple almost to severity, the chasteness of the design, the noble proportions and the characteristic disposition of what forms at once the structure and the ornament of the building are such as to produce a most imposing and pleasing effect. There is nothing wasted in decoration and enrichment, yet nothing wanting to satisfy the eye. In its very simplicity it bespeaks the genius of the designer as forcibly as a more elaborate work and will constitute another monument of the talent of the architect, Mr Chantrell'.

[25] Taylor was still in practice and seems to have commanded respect in the profession. However, his work frequently kept him away from Leeds and he built little in the town after Chantrell arrived.

[26] There is no indication as to the location of his residence at this time.

but by the beginning of 1821 he had moved to Bank Street.[27] He did not remain there for long and on 26 November he '. . . inform[ed] his friends and the public that he was removed from his house and office in Bank Street to Park Row, near the Philosophical Society Hall. N.B. his house and office in Bank Street to let'.[28] Park Row was part of the most fashionable area of the town yet was still convenient for its centre. His move there, to live with the more genteel members of the business and professional communities of the town as neighbours, was a clear statement of Chantrell's rising status.

In January 1823 Chantrell's professional position was enhanced by the foundation-stone laying for Christ Church, Leeds, which took place on the same day as that of Taylor's church at Quarry Hill. The two ceremonies were therefore turned into a single major event. It was arranged that '. . . a procession of the mayor and corporation, clergy of the parish, churchwardens, subscribers [for providing the sites], freemasons . . . to be formed at the Courthouse and proceed from thence to the Parish Church and after attending divine service to go to the [sites for the two churches]'.[29] A special place of honour was allotted to 'the architects, carrying their plans, and the plates'.[30] However, Chantrell's major success of 1823 lay in securing the commission to design the new South Market in Leeds, an important building in terms both of its cost, £23,000, and the quality of its design. This was Chantrell's third major public building in Leeds; since winning the Baths competition in 1819 he had received all the available commissions for important public buildings in the town. The market was part of a rapid expansion of retailing and commercial facilities which took place in Leeds in the mid 1820s, and, architecturally, it was the most exciting product of this expansion.[31] A public meeting held in the Court House on 16 June 1823 resolved 'that it is desirable that a public market shall be erected in the south division of this town . . .'.[32] With unusual haste, capital was raised, land purchased and only one week later, the *Intelligencer*

[27] The first known event at Bank Street occurs on 6 Jan. 1821 when he wrote to Soane.

[28] *LI*, 26 Nov. 1821. The last sentence is of interest and suggests that Chantrell was acting as agent for the re-letting of the premises.

[29] *LI*, 9 Jan. 1823.

[30] Beckwith, p.59.

[31] The economic and organisational background to this expansion is discussed thoroughly in K. Grady, 'The Provision of Markets in Leeds, 1822–29', *PTh.S*, LIV (1976), pp.165–95.

[32] *LI*, 19 June 1823.

invited 'architects, builders etc', to submit plans. Chantrell was announced as the appointed architect in the issue of 28 August 1823 which also stated that the building was to 'commence immediately'.

The finished structure consisted of a Cross for the sale of butter, eggs and poultry, twenty-three butchers shops and stalls, sixteen shops for miscellaneous purposes, eighty-eight stalls, nine slaughter-houses, and dwellings situated over eighteen of the shops (Plates 4(a)–5).[33] The accommodation requirements were, no doubt, outlined in the brief, since the design of Charles Fowler,[34] which was awarded the second prize, shows a similar range and quantity of accommodation. The comparison of the two designs helps to illustrate the high quality of Chantrell's scheme. The site is awkward and irregular; Fowler attempted to make his plan rectangular as far as it was possible, but Chantrell used the shape of the site as the basis of an imaginative layout. The design of Chantrell's shops are not in themselves especially noteworthy, but at the centre of his scheme was the Cross which was one of his most compelling designs (Plate 4(b)). Initially it was to be an open rotunda of two concentric circles of Greek Doric columns supporting a single pitched roof which probably had the whole of its central section open, or perhaps contained an oculus. The inspiration for this remarkable first design was almost certainly the Fish Market in Bruges, opened two years earlier in 1821 (Plate 6(a)). In the absence of any recent market buildings nearer to Leeds to serve as a model, it is not surprising that Chantrell should have been impressed by the Bruges market. In that example, the market's centrepiece is rectangular but, like Chantrell's design, has a double row of Doric columns supporting a single pitched roof around an open centre. In progressing from the Bruges model, and by detaching the centrepiece from the surrounding market structure, Chantrell's design is close in spirit, if not in scale, to the more advanced neo-Classicism usually associated with French and German designers. Perhaps it is to be regretted that this notable design was modified. The second, executed scheme was described thus:

> In the centre is a circular temple, intended for the Cross, composed of twelve Doric pillars outside and the same number inside. The outward ones support a bold entablature, where there is a reservoir for rain water; above rises a large cupola, used by the committee as a

[33] *LI*, 8 July, 1924.
[34] The plan is in TS, Box A.

place of meeting and for transacting other public
businesses connected with the market; it is enriched by
twelve small attached columns, and covered in with a
hemi-spherical headed dome, which originally contained
a machine for pumping water from an adjoining well
into the aforesaid reservoir.[35]

As a piece of hydraulic engineering, the building is also interesting.
The *Intelligencer* of 16 December 1824 noted that the 'machinery for
the cross is in progress and when the pump and fountains are added
it will be particularly attractive. The architect has further suggested
the advantage of the machine for watering the whole of the streets
and causeways during the dry summer months which may be
applied at a moderate expense'. Chantrell's 'bird's eye' view of the
scheme shows fountains at each side of the Cross but whether they
were ever built is not clear (Plate 4(a)). They are not mentioned in
the 1835 description[36] but this account does refer to there having
been a pumping machine in the dome.

During 1823 and 1824 there were numerous suggestions for
additional 'improvements'; 'scarcely a week elapses that we have
not had the pleasure to announce some project for improving and
adorning the town', stated the *Intelligencer*,[37] and Chantrell must
have entertained hopes that at least some of these proposed buildings
would be erected to his designs. Yet ironically, the success of the
South Market, a compelling and original composition, was not
repeated; never again did he build a new and permanent public
building, even though he remained in practice for a further twenty-
five years.

It appears to have been in 1824 that Chantrell's career received its
first setback. As part of the general desire to improve the marketing
and commercial facilities of the town, a covered market had been
first proposed in 1822 but it was not until April 1824 that plans for
this new building, to be called the Central Market, were called for.[38]
Apparently Chantrell's scheme was approved, although he was not
formally appointed. The point of conflict was that

> Mr Chantrell would not furnish working drawings . . .
> that injurious delay was the result, and that the
> Committee were compelled to apply to another quarter:

[35] Heaton, *Walk Through Leeds*, p. 102.
[36] *Ibid.*
[37] *LI*, 2 Dec. 1824.
[38] *Ibid.*, 22 April 1824.

> to which it is replied, that he in the outset had furnished
> all the Drawings, Plans, Estimates, etc. customary in
> such cases – that he only waited till he should be
> actually appointed the Architect, to furnish the Working
> Drawings – That the latter would have been very
> expensive, and that in no instance are they supplied
> before the Architect is chosen.[39]

On the face of it, there would seem to have been a misunderstanding
that could have been rectified. Since it was not resolved, one is left
to wonder whether there was not some more fundamental point of
conflict between the committee and Chantrell. Subsequently, Francis
Goodwin was appointed architect and the foundation stone of his
building was laid on 26 November 1824.[40]

During 1824, however, Chantrell was fully occupied with the
continuing work on Christ Church and the completion of the South
Market. Although he started no important new schemes, he
continued to receive publicity as the *Intelligencer* gave the public
periodical reports of the progress being made at the market and
church. For instance, 'With the South Market and the attraction
caused by the highly enriched Gothic church in Meadow Lane, both
executed from the designs and under the direction of Mr Chantrell,
this end of the town will be much enlivened . . .'.[41] Up to the time
of its dedication, Christ Church and its architect received regular
and unqualified praise from the *Intelligencer*. These comments
are all the more interesting in the context of the other two
'Commissioners' churches which were being built simultaneously
in Leeds: St Mary's, Quarry Hill, by Taylor; and St Mark's,
Woodhouse, by Sharp and Atkinson. These two churches and their
respective architects were not mentioned, except for the accounts
of such things as their foundation-stone layings or consecrations.

In the summer of 1824 there was a strike in the building trade in
Leeds but it is doubtful if it seriously disrupted any of Chantrell's
projects. Clearly he was on the side of the employers who were
trying to resist claims for higher wages, and he was quoted as having
said, 'There are five gentlemen who were on the point of
commencing building but who had instructed him to say that they

[39] *Ibid.*, 7 July 1825. This is a further example of the *Intelligencer*'s support for
Chantrell.
[40] *Ibid.*, 2 Dec. 1825.
[41] *Ibid.*, 27 May 1824.

would not proceed until the workmen had consented to work at the present price'.[42]

One can only speculate on the buildings these men had in mind, whether they did proceed with their projects or whether Chantrell had further disappointments. The wording of Chantrell's statement suggests these men were about to embark on private building projects and, if that is so, it is likely that at least some of them were houses. Certainly he was building one house in 1825, and that would seem to have been important as in April of that year he advertised for 'Joiners and Carpenters . . . for a large dwelling house about 1 mile from Leeds . . . cottages will be provided on the spot for such workmen as may require them at the customary rent'.[43] Chantrell is known to have erected houses for which tenders were not advertised, and it is likely that throughout his career he was building residences without any mention of them ever appearing in the pages of the papers.

Early in 1825 a number of architects were invited to submit designs for the proposed Commercial Buildings in Leeds, yet another manifestation of the expansion of business premises in the town. Six architects presented designs: Francis Goodwin, Anthony Salvin, Charles Barry, Thomas Taylor, John Clark and Chantrell.[44] The committee responsible for selecting an architect had difficulty in reaching its decision to appoint Clark, even after having, apparently, taken 'seven weeks' . . . to examine the schemes '. . . patiently and minutely . . .'.[45] The *Intelligencer* commented in detail on each scheme although it professed impartiality, saying 'none of [the designs] is free from objection or undeserving of praise . . .'.[46] Its remarks about Chantrell's scheme are interesting in that they illustrate the extent to which Chantrell's professional competence was being questioned at this time and show, once again, the invaluable support which the *Intelligencer* provided for him:

> . . . The remaining design is Mr Chantrell's; but before we attempt to specify either its defects or merits, we shall presume to advert to some rumours recently circulated respecting Mr Chantrell himself, which, unless disposed of, would render all remarks upon his

[42] *Ibid.*, 17 June 1824.
[43] *Leeds Mercury*, 16 April 1825.
[44] The *LI* of 15 Oct. 1829 stated that Thomas Harrison submitted a design but there is no mention of this elsewhere.
[45] *Ibid.*, 23 June 1825.
[46] *Ibid.*, 30 June 1825.

production a mockery. We come then broadly and directly to the point. It is stated, that some prejudice prevails against this gentleman for his professional conduct relative to the Philosophical Hall and the Central Market, and that in consequence, if his Design and Plans, etc. for the Commercial Buildings, were unexceptionable, they would still be rejected by the Subscribers at large, as well as by the Committee. Now if this be fact, may we not ask, without pretending to be Mr Chantrell's advocates, whether it would not have been fairer towards him and the Subscribers not to have invited him to send in a Design at all in the present case? Why solicit him to become a competitor for the prize, if, whatever his deserts, he was foredoomed never to obtain it? No gentleman surely could wish to make a scape-goat or a stalking-horse of one member of a profession for another or for others – and particularly at the expense of the Subscribers generally: for though disapproved of, Mr Chantrell's Design, like the rest of the unfortunate ones, must be paid for. We confess indeed that these reflections created at first a sort of conviction in our minds, that the report in question had no substantial foundation, and to satisfy ourselves, and be just to our readers, we enquired further into the matter. We have thus found that two distinct charges, enveloped in the usual atmosphere of general inculpation, are preferred against Mr Chantrell, and these charges, with Mr Chantrell's answers to them, are as follows. The first charge respects the Philosophical Hall, and assumes a double shape – namely that the expenditure much exceeded the estimate, and that owing to the Architect's negligence, the Joiner employed in one part of the building American Pine, instead of Memel timber. The answer to the former is, that the Committee for erecting the Hall, made great alterations in the Design, after it was, with its accompanying estimate approved of – and secondly, that in the progress of the work, they interfered without previously conferring with the Architect, and introduced further alterations to a considerable extent, by which the aggregate cost was swelled to a larger amount than originally set down. On the subject of the timber employed in the Philosophical Hall, Mr Chantrell alleges and the allegation is admitted on the other side, that he was the first to detect the American Pine, and that after three months contest, he succeeded in having it taken out of the building and Memel timber substituted. The other charge is that Mr Chantrell would not furnish working drawings for the

> Central Market . . . We think then, if nothing be
> extenuated or suppressed in the foregoing statement,
> that the prejudice towards Mr Chantrell is unfounded
> and unjust, and that any attempt to exclude him from a
> fair chance of the Commercial Buildings, on such
> grounds, ought to be resisted. Having said so much,
> however, upon the preceding, and in our opinion the
> material points as regards this gentleman, our criticism
> on his Design for that edifice must be extremely brief.
> Our chief objection to it externally is, that too florid an
> order of Architecture has been adopted, and that the
> ornaments are too numerous. In internal arrangement,
> the position of the Coffee-room relatively to the News
> Room, appears to us a striking defect. At the same time
> the general merits of the Design are so great, that we
> only regret our inability to do justice to them at
> present . . .[47]

The national boom of the first half of the 1820s, which had produced so much 'improvement' in Leeds and which promised even more, finally broke towards the end of 1825. The frequent accounts of expansionist projects which were to be found in the newspapers of 1823 and 1824 were replaced, in late 1825 and all of 1826, by accounts of bankruptcy. Not only were there no longer speculators or philanthropists eager to use their money for new buildings, but money that had been raised already for such projects was lost as banking houses suffered financial ruin. So far as the design of public buildings in Leeds was concerned, 1825 was a watershed; the depression effectively precluded further initiatives for new projects for a number of years, and when the economy recovered, and minds turned again to 'improvement', Taylor was dead and Chantrell's position as principal architect in the town was to be challenged by John Clark, the Edinburgh architect who won the Commercial Buildings competition and subsequently settled in Leeds.

During the course of the Central Market and Commercial Buildings competitions, it must have seemed to Chantrell that those eminent townsmen who had initially supported him could also make formidable enemies, but they did not abandon him totally. In April 1826 the council of the Philosophical and Literary Society voted to make alterations to their hall.[48] On 1 June the building

---

[47] *Ibid.*, 7 July 1825.
[48] *Ibid.*, 22 April 1826.

committee 'resolved that Mr Chantrell be appointed architect . . .
for the alterations on condition on entering into a bond to complete
the work for the estimated cost'.[49] However, at a subsequent meeting
the committee noted that 'Mr Chantrell having declined to enter
into a bond, Watson and Pritchett be applied to'.[50] Chantrell was a
member of the Society and, as architect of the building, he would
have been a logical choice to superintend alterations. However, to
have entered into a bond would have been a financial risk for him
and also an unusual stipulation for an architect to accept.
Furthermore, Chantrell was still in dispute with the Society over
his payment for the initial building; not only had he rejected
allegations of underestimating the cost of building the hall by
blaming the committe for requesting additions, but had stressed the
righteousness of his case by demanding an additional fee to cover
this extra work. It was never paid although Chantrell continued to
pursue the matter until at least 1830.[51]

One of the last schemes to escape the sudden recession was the
erection of a new Corn Exchange in Leeds. The otherwise almost
unknown architect Samuel Chapman won this competition despite
the endeavours of Goodwin and others.[52] In answer to rumours that
he had been an unsuccessful competitor, Taylor announced that his
ecclesiastical commissions had rendered him too busy to compete
for such an uncertain reward.[53] One wonders whether Chantrell
submitted a design or whether he, too, had become disenchanted
with the system of public competitions in which so much depended
on the whims and prejudices of the unqualified assessors.

In 1826 Chantrell's career took on a new direction. The facts are
clear; he produced no new permanent public buildings after the
South Market (completed 1824) and between 1826 and his removal
to London twenty years later, he designed or altered more than fifty
churches. The reasons for this change are more complex. It has been
shown already that Chantrell had suffered the frustrations and
uncertainties of competing for public buildings but by 1826 there
were not even competitions to enter. Perhaps it was the death of
Taylor in March 1826 that suggested this professional change of

[49] LUL, Papers of the Leeds Philosophical and Literary Society, MS. Dep. 1975/1,
    box 2/6: Building Committee Minute Book, 1819–27.
[50] Ibid.
[51] LUL, Papers of the Leeds Philosophical and Literary Society, MS. Dep. 1975/1,
    box 1/3: Council Minutes, 1822–40.
[52] LI, 8 Sept. 1825. Goodwin submitted a design but it is not known which other
    architects competed.
[53] Ibid., 8 Sept. 1825.

direction. Taylor and Chantrell were both products of a metropolitan architectural education in the late Georgian Classical tradition, but while Chantrell pursued the orthodox road to professional achievement through the designing of Classical public buildings, Taylor had demonstrated that the rather more unusual specialisation in the designing of Gothic churches could be equally lucrative and prestigious. It would seem to be clear from the letter he wrote to Soane in 1821[54] that Chantrell had not previously given much thought to the design of Gothic churches but Christ Church, Leeds, was widely admired. It has been suggested already that Chantrell was shrewd in securing professional advancement and he could have been well aware that Taylor's death presented him with the opportunity to succeed to the latter's ecclesiastical practice. Furthermore, Chantrell would have realised that the activities of the Parliamentary Commissioners would not be so susceptible to fluctuations in the economy.

Taylor's obituary notice in the *Intelligencer* records that he had 'made drawings for, and been appointed architect to the new churches at Manchester, Ripon and Almondbury'.[55] Whether Chantrell sought actively to succeed to some or all these commissions, or whether he was approached by either the local committee or the Commissioners in London, is not clear. However, by September 1826 the Commissioners had received a letter from the vicar of Almondbury which stated 'Mr Chantrell will soon furnish you with plans for Lockwood and Netherthong [churches]' (Plates 13(a) and 30).[56] In May 1827 the Commissioners 'requested [him] to go to [New Mills in the parish of] Glossop to view the site and prepare new designs'.[57] This is significant, as only occasionally did the Commissioners invite designs from a specific architect. It must have been only a few weeks later that Chantrell was asked by parishioners to survey, and subsequently rebuild, part of the old parish church at Glossop.[58] More than £1,000 had been spent repairing the church in 1822–26, but the work, carried out under the direction of Edward Drury of Sheffield,[59] had been done 'most injudiciously and . . . in very bad taste'.[60] and further work was necessary.

[54] SM, Private Correspondence, xv, A, 32.
[55] *LI*, 30 March 1826.
[56] At this time Lockwood and Netherthong were villages within the parish of Almondbury. The letter from the vicar is quoted in CBC MB 22, p.17.
[57] CBC MB 24, p.421.
[58] The application to the CBC for assistance in building the church was dated 8 May 1826: CBC, New Mills file, no. 18103.
[59] ICBS, 456 (Glossop).
[60] *Ibid.*, Chantrell's report of 19 June 1827.

The work carried out by Chantrell at New Mills and Glossop was, in many ways, unremarkable, and there were other architects who could have performed equally well. However, the incompetence demonstrated by Drury showed that there were also those who could not be relied on. It has been stated elsewhere that the Commissioners had no fixed idea about the stylistic treatment of the churches they paid for; what did concern them was the efficient management of the entire church building programme and the durability of individual churches. The principal qualities they sought in their architects were an ability to produce economical and durable designs, and the organisational skill to submit the necessary forms and drawings at the appropriate times. This is also true of the Incorporated Church Building Society, which was generally more involved with the repair of old churches than the building of new ones. Having discovered Chantrell's professional competence, both the Commissioners and the ICBS used his services extensively and, in a significant number of cases, where the commission involved solving problems that had already defeated other architects.

Soon after being asked to visit New Mills, Chantrell secured the appointments to build for the Commissioners the new church at Kirkstall, Leeds (Plate 13(b)), and early in the following year, 1828, they approved his designs for Morley (Plates 14(a) and (b)) and Holbeck, near Leeds (Plate 15(a)).

The esteem in which the Commissioners held him is underlined by the fact that when they were asked by the local committee at Horwich, Lancashire, for a suitable plan, they asked their surveyor, J. H. Good, to 'examine the drawings in the office to ascertain whether there be any design by Mr Chantrell applicable for the new church proposed to be erected at Horwich . . . to accommodate 1,500 persons . . .'.[61] However, Good replied that there appeared to be no design of Chantrell's for a church calculated to hold more than 1,000 persons.[62]

From 1826 to the end of 1831 much of Chantrell's time must have been devoted to the six new churches he built for the Commissioners, those at Lockwood, Netherthong (both near Huddersfield), New

---

[61] CBC MB 31, pp. 146–47.
[62] Whether subsequently Chantrell was asked to design such a church is not known, but one of this size was built there in 1830–31 to the design of Francis Bedford. The Commissioners also requested him to inspect a site in Hyde, Cheshire, intended for a new church, and to make proposals for the building. However, here also, Chantrell's scheme was not adopted: CBC MB 33 p. 145. In 1834 Chantrell wrote to the Commissioners requesting payment for plans and travelling as he had been asked by them to undertake the work: CBC, Hyde file.

Mills, Kirkstall, Morley and Holbeck. Also at this time he undertook repairs or alterations to the churches at Hunslet, Glossop, Woodhouse and Leeds; the first two of these were paid for, in part, by the ICBS, and he submitted designs, which were not executed, for proposed churches at Bramley and Hyde. Chantrell was not, however, absolutely consistent in his use of Gothic for ecclesiastical commissions: in 1830 he added to Hunslet Chapel – a plain Georgian structure – a remarkable tower in the manner of Soane (Plate 6(b)). Neither, during this period, did he altogether abandon secular commissions: in February 1827 he produced designs for an enlargement of the Court House in Leeds (Plates 7(a) and (b)), which was eventually carried out in 1834, and in 1828 he supervised alterations to the Leeds Library.

But although one might have expected that a pupil of Soane would have seen country house commissions as an important ingredient in a successful career, there is documentary evidence to support his authorship of only two such projects, Armitage Bridge House, near Huddersfield (Plate 8(b)), and Rudding Park, near Harrogate; there is no evidence that he sought appointments to design other large houses but had his proposals rejected. He designed Armitage Bridge House in 1828. This is a modest-sized dwelling by country house standards but included a service wing, stables and out-offices. The main block is an orthodox, but soundly composed five-bay, two-storey classical villa. The house was built for members of the Brooke family who owned the nearby mill, and who were staunch supporters of the Church of England. It was from Armitage Bridge House that the procession began for the first stone-laying ceremony of the new church at Lockwood. It is not known if members of the Brooke family were members of the 'local committee' in the Almondbury parish but it seems highly likely that Chantrell's appointment to design the churches at Lockwood and Netherthong led to the Armitage Bridge House commission. During the following twenty years Chantrell designed a number of other buildings for the Brookes.

Although Chantrell undertook a considerable amount of work at Rudding Park, the project was concerned essentially with repairs. The house was described in 1818 as a 'spacious modern mansion recently erected',[63] and although it is possible that it was not completed at this date, it was certainly sufficiently finished to be inhabited. In 1824, it was bought by Sir Joseph Radcliffe and subsequently major repairs were necessary as a result of an outbreak

[63] *LI*, 18 Aug. 1818.

of dry rot. 'It appears evident that the infection was communicated by some of the oak timbers of the old mansion, which was taken down because of dry-rot, having been used with the new wood, probably from their sound appearance.'[64]

Chantrell was certainly engaged in the dry-rot eradication at Rudding Park in 1834,[65] but the dates on which he began and finished the commission are not known. His undated abstract of the tradesmen's bills,[66] which is incomplete, shows a total cost of £11,047. Since the entire house could have been built for about £20,000,[67] Chantrell's task must have been to do more than remove the decayed timbers. The abstract includes more than £2,500 for masonry and perhaps Chantrell extended or significantly remodelled the structure.

A commission to eradicate dry-rot, even if it was part of a more inspiring engagement, was a long way from 'architecture' as interpreted by the Royal Academy. However, the possession of this sort of practical knowledge could be a valuable attribute, and it was by no means common to all architects. From 1835, following the successful completion of the Rudding commission, Chantrell received a number of appointments[68] from the Church Building Commissioners which entailed the repair of churches only a few years old in which dry-rot had developed, due to either poor design or inadequate supervision of the builders. In either event, the fault lay with the architect of the building, but it was to Chantrell that the Commissioners turned for assistance, rather than the churches' designers.

It is perhaps reasonable to see the period 1831–37 as something of a trough in the course of Chantrell's career. In 1831 he finished the last of the six new churches begun in the previous decade, and in 1837 he was appointed to rebuild the parish church in Leeds. Between these two events there were few prestigious commissions and the largest of them, in terms of cost, Rudding Park, was an

---

[64] CBC, Cleckheaton file, no. 15199.
[65] LCA, Radcliffe of Rudding, II/399: Chantrell to Radcliffe, 22 Aug. 1834. Chantrell refers to his work at Rudding in a report on Birkenshaw church: CBC Cleckheaton file.
[66] Radcliffe of Rudding, II/400.
[67] For instance, Lough Crew, an Irish house of about the same size as Rudding, cost over £22,000 in the late 1820s: D. Watkin, *The Life and Work of C. R. Cockerell* (1974), p. 168.
[68] These were: St Paul's, Birkenshaw in 1835; St John's, Cleckheaton in 1840; St John's, Dewsbury Moor in 1839–40; St Peter's, Earlsheaton in 1840; and St James's, Heckmondwike, also in 1840.

isolated appointment in that it did not lead to similar engagements elsewhere.

By this time John Clark had settled in Leeds and deposed Chantrell from the position of leading architect in the town. Clark was undeniably skilled at handling the classical repertoire and in the 1830s secured an impressive number of commissions for public buildings and suburban mansions in which he displayed this ability. However, he was less accomplished when dealing with the Gothic style and perhaps this served to confirm the reorientation of Chantrell's career from the secular to the ecclesiastical. Yet in the mid 1830s there were few commissions for new churches for him to pursue; the funds of the Church Building Commission were almost exhausted and rarely could the erection of a church be financed by private subscription. Limited funds meant that the ever-present problem of insufficient church accommodation could usually be tackled only by the repair of old churches to prolong their life, in conjunction with an extension or internal rearrangement to provide additional seats. In this category belong Chantrell's commissions at All Saints, Glossop (1827–32); St Oswald's, Guiseley (1830–33); All Saints, Pontefract (1831–32) (Plate 16(a)); Armley Chapel (1833–34) (Plate 15(b)); and Bramley Chapel (1833) (Plate 16(b)). Also at this time he added galleries to two recently-built churches, St Marks, Leeds (1832–33 and 1836–37) and his own Christ Church, Leeds (1836). His major ecclesiastical commission of the mid 1830s was Christ Church, Skipton (1835–39) (Plates 17(a) and (b)), a building of national importance because of its pioneering internal arrangements. Chantrell designed only one other new church in this period, St Michael's, Headingley (1836–38) where he was compelled to work within a budget of only £2,500 (Plate 18(a)).[69]

In 1829 he designed the school attached to St Mary's, Quarry Hill, Leeds (Plate 3(b)). This was followed by a number of other schools, vicarages and almshouses, which together form an interesting group of buildings. All of them were built cheaply and they are architecturally unexciting. They are predominantly simple, box-like structures and are nominally 'Gothic' in style. The decoration tends to be confined to plain arched windows and doors with a moulded drip over them. However, at a time when other commissions were not numerous, they must have formed a useful source of income and this type of building was a logical extension of Chantrell's ecclesiastical Gothic practice. The group includes a school and almshouses at Armley in 1832, a school attached to

[69] *Gentleman's Magazine*, 1839, p.532.

St Peter's, Morley, of 1832–33, an enlargement of St Mark's School, Feather Hill, Leeds in 1832, a vicarage at Kirkstall in 1834–35 (Plate 13(b)), a school at Armitage Bridge in 1835, a school attached to St Matthew's, Holbeck in 1839 and a school attached to Christ Church, Leeds in 1839–42.[70] It is interesting to note how many of these buildings were associated with churches or other buildings that Chantrell had worked on previously and which, one assumes, had earned him esteem in the various localities.

Chantrell's known secular commissions of the mid 1830s suggest that he had almost ceased to pursue this type of appointment and the minor alterations which he supervised at the Leeds Library in 1835 probably resulted from the Library committee approaching him, since they had employed him in a similar capacity in the previous decade.

To a certain extent, the 1830s saw a recovery from the economic depression of the mid 1820s, and this brought with it opportunities for the erection of additional public buildings. In Leeds these included a new General Cemetery in 1833, a new Workhouse in 1835, a proposed new Corn Exchange in 1836 and a proposed new Borough Gaol in 1837. Clark won the Cemetery competition, Chantrell's entry not even being short-listed. Perhaps he believed that the prejudice from which he suffered in the mid 1820s still existed, and thus felt it was pointless to compete for the Workhouse commission, for which he was not among the twelve entrants.[71] Whether any designs by him were among 'nearly 50 plans submitted for the Corn Exchange'[72] and whether he presented a design for the Gaol is not known.

In the context of Clark's other successes with Classical schemes, it could have been anticipated that he would defeat Chantrell in the Cemetery competition, despite the latter having produced a design which 'suggested such arrangements as were usual in the days of the Romans'.[73] However it must have been even more depressing for Chantrell, and seemed more serious for his career in the long term, to have been beaten into second place by Clark in 1836, in the competition for the new church which became St George's, Mount Pleasant, Leeds. Clark's Gothic churches are undistinguished and his scheme for St George's is no exception. Worse still for Chantrell

---

[70] For the buildings at Armley, Morley and Armitage Bridge there is no known documentation and they are attributed to Chantrell on the basis of style and their close proximity to documented works of his.

[71] *LI*, 14 March 1835.

[72] *Ibid.*, 13 Feb. 1836.

[73] LUL, MS.421/140/1: Leeds General Cemetery Papers.

PLATE 9 (a)   LEEDS: HOLY TRINITY, DESIGNED
BY WILLIAM ETTY, 1722–27.
Engraving by Whittock and Rogers, 1828.

PLATE 9 (b)   LEEDS: HOLY TRINITY, DESIGNED BY
WILLIAM ETTY, 1722–27.
The top three stages of the tower were added by
Chantrell in 1839.

PLATE 10 (a)   LEEDS: CONSERVATIVE PAVILION, 1838.
From a watercolour, perhaps by Chantrell.

PLATE 10 (b)   LEEDS: YORKSHIRE AGRICULTURAL SOCIETY PAVILION, 1839.

PLATE 11 (b)   LEEDS: CHRIST CHURCH, 1821–26.

PLATE 11 (a)   BRAMLEY, LEEDS: CHAPEL.
Unexecuted design for enlargement, 1823.
Drawing by Chantrell.

PLATE 12 (a)   ARMLEY, LEEDS: CHAPEL, PROPOSED EXTENSION *c*. 1823–25.
Drawing by Chantrell.

PLATE 12 (b)   DESIGNS BY C. A. BUSBY (OR FRANCIS GOODWIN) FOR INTENDED
CHURCHES AT OLDHAM AND LEEDS, 1821.

PLATE 13 (a)   LOCKWOOD, NEAR HUDDERSFIELD: EMMANUEL 1826–30.

PLATE 13 (b)   KIRKSTALL, LEEDS: ST STEPHEN, 1827–29, PARSONAGE 1834–35.
Watercolour by W. B. Robinson, 1849.

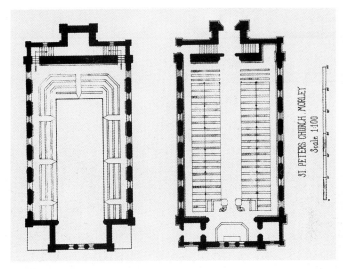

ST PETERS CHURCH, MORLEY
Scale 1:100

PLATE 14 (b)   MORLEY, NEAR LEEDS: ST PETER, 1828–30.
Plans, drawn by the author.

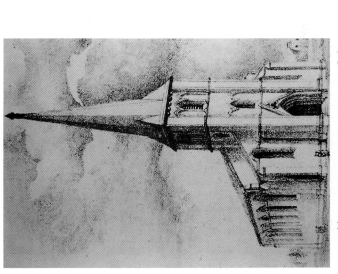

PLATE 14 (a)   MORLEY, NEAR LEEDS: ST PETER, 1828–30.
From a nineteenth century lithograph.

PLATE 15 (a)   HOLBECK, LEEDS: ST MATTHEW, 1827–32.
Watercolour by N. R. Robinson.
Chantrell intended the tower to have a spire, but it had to be abandoned due to a
shortage of funds. The present spire – rather more elaborate than that intended by
him – was added in the mid nineteenth century.

PLATE 15 (b)   ARMLEY, LEEDS: CHAPEL.
Drawing by Chantrell showing his proposed additions and alterations of 1833–34.

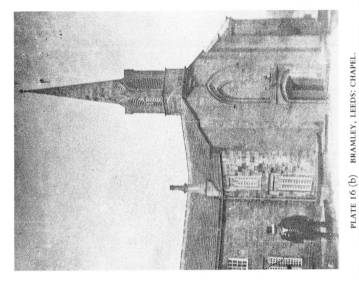

PLATE 16 (b)   BRAMLEY, LEEDS: CHAPEL.
Copy of an old photograph showing Chantrell's addition of
a south 'transept' of 1833.

PLATE 16 (a)   PONTEFRACT, WR: ALL SAINTS.
Lithograph by Inchbold, 1831, showing Chantrell's scheme to
restore the interior, 1831–33.

was the fact that Clark's design was a pastiche of some of the former's own executed designs of ten years earlier.

In 1821, Chantrell had moved to a building in Park Row, which he used as both his residence and office.[74] The 1826 directory[75] is more specific, and gives his address as 1, Park Row, probably the property into which he moved five years earlier. By 1830, when the next directory appeared, his office had moved to 11 and 12, Benson's Buildings, 2, Park Row,[76] and in July 1833 he removed his place of residence to a house called *Oatlands*, in the northern suburbs, while maintaining his office in Benson's Buildings.[77] He continued to live at *Oatlands* until he removed to London although he ceased to have an office in Benson's Buildings some years earlier. *Oatlands* was an unlikely residence for a successful architect; it was not designed by its inhabitant, it did not conform to any of the fashionable architectural styles of the period, and it was not old enough to have been of interest to an antiquarian. It was, in fact, a rather rambling and architecturally unpretentious house of perhaps eighteenth-century date. Subsequent additions had produced a substantial house whose scale and visual features were those of a cottage. There is no evidence that Chantrell made any alterations to it. A situation in Camp Road, on the northern side of Leeds, would have been respectable, but it was too close to the centre of the town to have been included in the most fashionable suburbs further north, such as Headingley.

During the 1830s Chantrell became more conspicuous in local affairs. The *Intelligencer* of 20 January 1831 carried a letter to the editor from him concerning 'the late fire in Commercial Street' in which great damage was caused. He made a number of sensible suggestions for improving fire precautions which included the placing of taps at regular intervals beneath the pavements so that firemen might have easy access to a supply of water. In July 1831 the Leeds Gas Light Company appealed against the rates levied on them by the Overseers. Subsequently, a small group of architects, land surveyors, solicitors, etc., was asked to value the property, and the architectural profession was represented by Chantrell and Lees Hammerton.[78] At the end of 1834 Chantrell stood for election to the Leeds Improvement Commission, a body which was

---

[74] *LI*, 26 Nov. 1821.
[75] E. Parsons, *General and Commercial Directory of the Borough of Leeds* (Leeds, 1826), p.27.
[76] E. Parsons, and W. White, *Directory of the Borough of Leeds* (Leeds, 1830), p.127.
[77] *LI*, 27 July 1833.
[78] *Ibid.*, 7 July 1831.

responsible for public health and safety, and elementary civic facilities in the borough. He became one of nineteen commissioners elected to serve for 1835,[79] and during that year business was concerned principally with the building of a waterworks. He took the chair at the Commission's session of 5 March,[80] but was often absent from meetings, and is not reported as having said anything of note at those he did attend. By the middle of the year he had ceased to play any part in the Commission's activities, perhaps from a feeling of frustration at the group's inability to make progress – a criticism voiced frequently in the *Intelligencer* at this time. He did not apply for re-election at the close of 1835. On 20 May 1837 the *Intelligencer* announced that it was proposed to establish Zoological and Botanical Gardens in Leeds, and in the following week noted that Chantrell was both a shareholder in the enterprise and a member of the provisional committee to manage the garden's affairs. In December of that year he was elected to its council.[81]

Chantrell found time to visit the Continent during the summer but it cannot have been an extensive tour; he visited the ICBS's office in London on 8 August 'when returning from the continent', having previously called at their office on 17 July.[82] Given this limited period of time, it is possible that he went only to Bruges to visit his relations. Since he was prepared, on this occasion, to undertake the journey abroad and stay for such a short time, it is possible that this is only one of a number of visits he made there.

In the autumn of 1837 Chantrell began a project which was to revitalise his flagging career and transform his professional status. This was the rebuilding of St Peter's, the old parish church of Leeds (Plates 25(a)–29(b)), the impetus for which came from the newly-appointed vicar, Dr Walter Farquhar Hook. He began his appointment on 15 April 1837, and immediately turned his attention to the physical state of the church, so that only two weeks later the *Intelligencer* was able to announce proposed improvements.[83] By the beginning of October that year Hook was envisaging more extensive alterations and on 19 October he had a meeting with a group of leading gentlemen of the town to discuss how best to proceed. So

[79] *Ibid.*, 3 Jan. 1835.
[80] *Ibid.*, 7 March 1835.
[81] *Ibid.*, 23 Dec. 1837.
[82] ICBS, 1337 (Holmbridge).
[83] *LI*, 29 April 1837.

far the vicar was working without any professional architectural advice, but clearly the services of an architect were to become necessary as the scheme reached a more detailed stage of planning. As a recent arrival in Leeds, it is unlikely that the vicar knew the local architectural talent, and at the meeting on 19 October it was John Gott who suggested Chantrell for the work at the parish church. Considering Clark's superior status in the town plus the fact that, only the year before, he had been appointed to design St George's, it is perhaps surprising that he was not engaged at the parish church. On the other hand, it should be remembered that at this stage it was envisaged that the restoration was to be relatively cheap and involve no more expense than was necessary to increase the accommodation, and restore a sense of decency to the chancel. Clearly Chantrell was the more experienced architect at this sort of commission which required ingenuity with constructional problems, and a sympathetic blending of the new work with the old. However, if, from the beginning, it had been intended virtually to build a new church as an expensive and prestigious project, is it possible that Clark rather than Chantrell would have been appointed?

The rebuilding of Leeds Parish Church led to numerous other ecclesiastical commissions. The building of the oratory in the graveyard of the parish church in 1838, and in the same year, alterations to St John's, Leeds, to increase its accommodation, were a direct result of the need to close the parish church while the restoration was in progress. In addition, Chantrell repaired St John's, Adel, in 1838–39 (Plate 20(a)), rebuilt St Wilfrid's, Pool, near Leeds, in 1838–40, repaired Christ Church, Leeds, in 1839, rebuilt the tower of Holy Trinity, Leeds, in 1839, altered St Matthew's, Chapel Allerton, in 1839–40 and built a new church at Batley Carr, near Batley, in 1839–41. Further afield he designed churches for Lothersdale, near Skipton, in 1838 and Farnley Tyas, in the parish of Almondbury, in 1838–40.

On 19 July 1839 the roof and part of the tower of Bruges Cathedral were destroyed by fire, and among those invited to tender for the necessary restoration was William Chantrell, R. D. Chantrell's brother, who was a successful businessman in Bruges, and had some experience of civil engineering, and perhaps architecture. On being appointed to repair the cathedral, he enlisted the help of his brother from Leeds, and in so doing probably made him the first English architect to work on a Continental cathedral. The cathedral archives recorded that 'it was [R. D. Chantrell] who as architect directed the reconstruction of the roofs'[84] which probably means he supplied the designs, and W. D. Chantrell acted as 'entrepreneur' or contractor. The roof was finished by June 1840, and R. D. Chantrell had certainly visited the city at some time between the fire and this date: there is a drawing by him of the cathedral showing the proposed extension to the tower, which would seem to have been made while standing in front of the building, and this is dated September 1839. However, the exact date of his visit or visits during this project is not known (Plate 21(b)).

So far, Chantrell's secular work was, with the possible exception of the South Market's first design, competent but unremarkable, and, given his training, predictable. Its style and range was typical of an accomplished provincial late Georgian architect. However, by c.1840 this aspect of his career had taken on a rather different character and thus, from the very beginning of Victoria's reign, he could be seen as a typical 'Victorian' architect, with a range of stylistic, technological and professional skills which the term implies.

In 1838 he produced a design for a 'Tudor' gatelodge for the 'estate belonging to the late John Atkinson Esq's trustees'[85] in the Clarendon Road area of Leeds (Plate 8(a)). It seems not to have been built. The design shows a single-storey building. Its main elevation is symmetrical, of three bays, with the centre one projecting. In this is the door, set in a Tudor arch, with a drip mould over it and surmounted by a shaped gable containing a projecting lozenge. The side bays contain simple two-light 'Tudor' windows. The four corners of the building are denoted by pinnacles as is the apex of the gables on the side elevations. It is Chantrell's first known Tudor building and shows how he could turn his hand to an unfamiliar style, yet handle the necessary components competently. Furthermore, he did this at a time when the style was just beginning to enter the mainstream of English architecture, and when there were relatively few models from which he could have copied.[86]

---

[84] Diocese of Bruges, Cathedral Archives, *Resolutions of the Church Wardens*, 5 April 1849–31 Dec. 1850. The information about Chantrell's contribution is written in the margin of the report of the Ceremony of Thanksgiving, on 7 July 1849, when the roof was finished. Further information about this commission can be found in A. Van den Abeele, 'Entrepreneurs brugeois au XIX siècle', pp.239–66.

[85] The drawing is in LCA, DB 5/23, Atkinson family papers.

[86] The style was becoming popular for country houses during the 1830s and much work in this style was undertaken by Edward Blore. Around the middle of the nineteenth century many of the larger houses in the Headingley area of Leeds used this style.

Chantrell's versatility is further demonstrated in the spire he designed and built for Holy Trinity church, Leeds, the following year.[87] On 2 February 1839 the *Intelligencer* reported that the spire of the church had again suffered storm damage, but that repairs carried out under Chantrell's supervision had rendered it safe until the weather improved sufficiently for it to be taken down.

The church was begun in 1723 to the design of William Etty of York.[88] An engraving of the church published in 1816[89] shows the tower consisting of two stages rising above the roof of the church, each of which has pairs of pilasters in the corners. On top of the tower was a spire (Plate 9(a)). This topmost section was not part of the original design but was an 'early addition' to the tower.[90] The spire did not harmonise with the tower and, it seems, was not well liked.[91] The storm damage necessitated its removal and in its place Chantrell built an additional three stages to the tower, each reduced in area from the one below it (Plate 9(b)). The source is unmistakable: it is a pastiche of the towers of James Gibbs which were illustrated in his *A Book of Architecture* of 1728. This 'borrowing' was entirely appropriate; the Gibbs designs were produced at about the same time as Etty's and, in a number of ways, the body of Holy Trinity is similar to that of Gibbs's St Martin-in-the-Fields, London. However, it is of some interest that Chantrell's additional stages were built at all since the removal of the spire would have left the tower looking reasonably complete, and in this form it would have been similar to a number of other eighteenth-century Classical towers in Yorkshire. Since Chantrell supervised the emergency repairs to the spire, it seems reasonable to assume that he was involved from the beginning in discussions about its replacement. At a time when it was widely believed that Classicism was unsuitable for churches and when Baroque was the least acceptable of the Classical styles, it could have been expected that the tower would have been left in as discreet a form as was possible. However, Chantrell did just the opposite; the addition is a positive celebration of Baroque and even exploits the possibilities of the style more fully than did the original structure. One can almost sense that Chantrell revelled in this rare opportunity to display his talents as a designer

---

[87] Because of its stylistic implications, the design of Holy Trinity spire is discussed here rather than with other ecclesiastical commissions in Chapter 4.

[88] Linstrum, p.186. An illustration of Etty's design appears in W. J. Connor, 'The Architect of Holy Trinity Church, Leeds', *PTh.S*, LIV (1977), p.297.

[89] T. D. Whitaker (ed.), *Loidis and Elmete* (1816), facing p.65.

[90] H. W. Thompson, *A Short Account of Holy Trinity, Leeds* (Leeds, 1927), p.14.

[91] Whitaker, *Loidis and Elmete*, quoted in Linstrum, p.186, fn. 6.

in the Classical tradition. The result is one of his most successful designs; the addition harmonises with the original yet enhances it at the same time. It is perhaps unique as an example of early Victorian architecture which has been consistently admired and valued for its contribution to the Leeds skyline. Like the gatelodge for John Atkinson's estate, the tower for Holy Trinity represented a new style for Chantrell and, again, shows that he had the confidence and breadth of knowledge to design in a style that had not yet come to be widely used by his contemporaries.[92]

In the late 1830s it is possible to detect signs of a warming of relations between Chantrell and the principal townsmen of Leeds who, collectively, seemed to have been prejudiced against him for more than a decade. The first sign of the thaw comes in Chantrell's appointment at the parish church and, perhaps as a token of goodwill on his part, the following year he gratuitously offered to design a temporary pavilion for the Leeds Tradesmen's Conservative Association's third annual dinner. Having been defeated in 1835, in the first municipal elections following the Municipal Corporation Reform Act, the Conservatives were anxious to reassert themselves, and the 1838 dinner was intended to be a conspicuous symbol of the party's importance. The pavilion became a focus of Conservative pride, and a useful way for Chantrell to ingratiate himself with this influential group (Plate 10(a)).

As a temporary structure, the pavilion marks yet another new area into which Chantrell was moving at this time. In the absence of any existing building capable of accommodating a large assembly[93], it was decided to '. . . make arrangements for accommodating 1,500 persons in a handsome pavilion to be erected for that purpose . . .'[94] on a piece of vacant land in Park Row, Leeds.[95] The pavilion was to be the venue for the celebratory dinner and, at the end of the week of festivities, the 'Grand Conservative Ball'.

When it is considered that, at about the same time, St Wilfrid's, Pool, was built for £308[96] the cost of the pavilion, £600,[97] seems

---

[92] C. R. Cockerell is a notable exception to this statement. See D. Watkins, *The Life and Work of C. R. Cockerell* (1974).

[93] Large public dinners were occasionally held in the Music Hall during this period but the diners were divided among a number of rooms and the total accommodation is unlikely to have been adequate for the Conservatives' needs.

[94] *LI*, 24 March 1838.

[95] *Ibid.*

[96] ICBS, 2028 (Pool): part of the old structure was reused which helped to keep the cost so small.

[97] The cost is given on the drawing in the RIBA Drawing Collection, J8/20. The *LI* of 24 March 1838 noted that the building work 'was contracted for £395'.

extravagant for a temporary structure. However, the pavilion was intended to be a conspicuous symbol of Conservative pride and authority. The building had

> . . . a Grecian exterior [with] . . . a Hexagonal Portico in Antis, which is surmounted by a pediment bearing the Royal Arms . . . within the portico is a spacious hall, leading, on the left, to the Gentlemen's room adjoining the Saloon and the Ladies Cloak Room communicating with the Gallery. On the right of the entrance hall is the Receiver's Room for Tickets, Waiters' Apartments, Bar, Scullery, Pantries etc. The Saloon is 120 feet long, by 80 feet broad . . . the Gallery will comfortably accommodate 500 ladies . . . and the interior walls of the Saloon will be lined with white calico and the pillars and pilasters painted deep crimson . . . The effect will be similar to the interiors described in the accounts of Pompeii and Herculanium and the exterior wall will be coloured to represent Greek Polychromatic Painting. The whole of the edifice will be of timber and plank, framed together in the most secure and substantial manner . . . for the entire design of this truly chaste and classical building, the inhabitants of Leeds and the gentry of the County are indebted to Robt Dennis Chantrell Esq. Arch. of this town, who has, in the most handsome manner gratuitously offered to the committee his valuable services.[98]

There is no evidence to suggest that the building could be dismantled, stored, and subsequently re-erected. However, the following year Chantrell designed another temporary pavilion, on this occasion for the Yorkshire Agricultural Society (Plate 10(b)). Its form was similar to the one for the Conservatives, but the dimensions are different and illustrations suggest these were two quite independent buildings.

There are other indications that at this time Chantrell sought to capitalise on his recently improved standing in the town. On 21 June 1838 he became a member of the masonic Lodge of Fidelity in Leeds,[99] after having joined a Wakefield Lodge the year before.[100] The following

---

[98] *LI*, 31 March 1838. The description of the building was written by Chantrell: *LI* 18 April 1833. The enthusiasm for the building, which is apparent in this article in a Tory paper, needs to be balanced by the criticism to be found in the Liberal *Leeds Mercury*, which described it as 'the Rat Trap' and encouraged rumours about its inability to support the weight of 1,500 people.

[99] A. Scarth and C. A. Brain, *History of the Lodge of Fidelity* (Leeds, 1894), p.220.

[100] Chantrell joined the Lodge of Unanimity on 26 June 1837: ex inf. Mr John Goodchild, Wakefield.

year the breach between Chantrell and the Philosophical and Literary Society seems to have been healed, for in April Chantrell gave a lecture to the Society entitled 'An Historical Account of the late Parish Church in Leeds, with some Observations relating to ancient fragments discovered during the removal of various parts of the building'.[101] This indicates not only that Chantrell was perhaps courting yet another important section of the townsmen, but also the extent to which the building work at the parish church had created interest beyond its ecclesiastical significance. On 15 March 1839 the Society's council proposed remodelling the museum and 'resolved that the Curator be requested to obtain plans and specifications of the projected alterations'.[102] Perhaps his lecture of the following month was a sufficient sign of penitence on Chantrell's part, and on 17 May 'Mr Teale [the Curator] . . . laid before the Council the plan by Mr Chantrell . . .'.[103] In November he was re-elected a member of the Society,[104] after a lapse of more than twelve years, and in the Society's *Report for the Session 1839–40* '. . . thanks were voted to Mr Chantrell for his gratuitous services in planning and superintending the improvements . . .'.[105] In March 1840 Chantrell delivered a lecture on Italian architecture,[106] in April 1842 he spoke to them on Gothic architecture,[107] and in April 1843 his subject was the 'Geometric Principles of Gothic Architecture'.[108] Also in 1843, he designed the 'classical and appropriate' pedestal for Parkes's statue of M. T. Sadler which was placed in the Hall.[109]

The *Intelligencer* of 13 May 1839 announced that there was to be 'The Leeds Public Exhibition' which would open in July of that year. It was to be a display of 'works of art, objects illustrative of general and practical science etc', and Chantrell, who was a member of the committee, lent a selection of his own possessions for the Exhibition. These included specimens of stone carving of AD 1150, 1240 and 1350, a model of Headingley new church,[110] and drawings of fragments of

[101] *LI*, 13 April 1839. The lecture was given on 19 April.
[102] Leeds Philosophical and Literary Society, Council Minutes, 1822–40.
[103] *Ibid.*
[104] *LI*, 9 Nov. 1839.
[105] *Ibid.*, 2 May 1840.
[106] *Ibid.*, 14 March 1840.
[107] Leeds Philosophical and Literary Society, *Annual Report*, 1841–42.
[108] *LI*, 15 April 1843.
[109] *Ibid.*, 21 May 1843.
[110] Also in the exhibition were a number of architectural models, including one of the Headingley old chapel, made by R. W. Moore, who was at this time a pupil of Chantrell. It is thus likely that Moore made the Headingley new church model, and it would be interesting to know how many other Chantrell buildings had models made of them.

an ancient cross and other relics found in the walls of Leeds parish church.[111] It seems that he contributed the drawings of the cross, or perhaps the stones themselves, to the 'Bradford Exhibition' in 1840,[112] and for the Leeds Public Exhibition of 1843 he lent further pieces from his collection. These included a 'Dress Sword with a chased silver hilt', fragments of stained and painted glass from the old parish church, Roman mortar from York, petrified wood from Belgium and copper and silver coins.[113]

Chantrell joined the Institute of British Architects as a Fellow in 1836, two years after its inception, and, throughout the remainder of his stay in Leeds, he was the town's only architect to have FIBA after his name. The professionalism which this implied was important in an age when anyone could practise as an architect, regardless of talent or honesty, and gave an added dimension to his status, as the following two events illustrate. First, in 1840 he was asked to adjudicate a dispute between John Atkinson of Little Woodhouse and J. Collinson, a stonemason, concerning the amount that the latter should be paid for some paving work.[114] Second, in 1843, during the first service at the new church at Farsley, near Leeds, designed by William Wallen, 'great alarm was caused that the gallery was giving way'. Wallen came to inspect the structure,

> and was convinced that all was secure but for the satisfaction and assurance of the public he recommended that R. D. Chantrell Esq, a gentleman entirely unconnected with the building, should be requested to inspect the work and give his unbiased opinion. Mr Chantrell, with his uniform kindness at once repaired to the church and gave the following report . . . [which agreed with Wallen's assessment that everything was sound].[115]

By the 1840s there was an established and increasing interest on the part of the middle and upper classes in 'English Antiquities': there was popular interest in the crosses found in the walls of the old Leeds parish church; and the Norman church at Adel, the roof of which Chantrell restored in 1843, was an object of curiosity. That he was seen as an expert in archaeology, especially that of the middle

---

[111] *Catalogue of the Leeds Public Exhibition, 1839.*
[112] The *Intelligencer*, of 10 Oct. contains a long letter from Chantrell in which he defends his suggestion that the fragments of the Cross are pre-Saxon.
[113] *Catalogue of the Leeds Public Exhibition, 1843.*
[114] LCA, DB 5/41: Atkinson family papers.
[115] *LI*, 4 Nov. 1843.

ages, was an important addition to his reputation as an architect of modern buildings. The professionalism which he displayed in his practice, and his credible archaeological scholarship, was a combination which made him unique among the architects of the region. Indeed, in 1843 the Bishop of Ripon was to refer to him as 'one of the first architects in all the north of England'.[116]

These various professional advantages brought Chantrell a considerable quantity of work in the 1840s; in 1840 alone he was working on at least twenty different commissions, a list of which reveals not only the quantity of his output but its variety in terms of style and building types.[117] When it is remembered that twenty-two days had been devoted to the design of Holmbridge church,[118] and that, had the scheme been executed, there would have been a substantial addition to this time for supervision of the building work, it is possible to gain an idea of the number of hours per week which were needed for running the practice in 1840. This was surely his busiest year, but for most of the rest of his period of residence in Leeds he was engaged in more commissions than in earlier years. Given this demand for his services, one might have expected that Chantrell would have been selective in the commissions he accepted, yet when his career was at its busiest, he continued to accept appointments which were neither lucrative nor prestigious, and which it is hard to believe offered him any sort of personal satisfaction either. These commissions included repairs, often caused by dry-rot, to churches designed by other architects in the 1820s, and Chantrell seems to have made something of a speciality of this sort of work. That it was necessary at all is indicative of the variable quality of the architects practising in the early nineteenth century, and Chantrell's skill in overcoming the problems encountered is a further example of his practical ability.

An examination of his commissions of c.1840 gives a clear indication of the sheer range of his output. He was engaged on

---

[116] CBC, Golcar file, no. 26725.
[117] These are: Leeds Parish Church, 1837–41; new church at Farnley Tyas, 1838–40; new church at Pool, 1838–40; alterations to St Matthew's, Chapel Allerton, 1839–40; new church at Batley Carr, 1839–41; new church at Cowling, 1839–45; reflooring St John's, Cleckheaton, 1839–40; re-roofing of Bruges Cathedral, 1839–40; new school at Holbeck, 1839–40; repairs to St John's, Dewsbury Moor, 1840; repairs to St Peter's, Earlsheaton, 1840; repairs to Holy Trinity, Leeds, 1840–41; new church at Honley, 1840–43; alterations to the Music Hall, Leeds, 1840; repairs to St James's, Heckmondwike, 1840; new school, Hunslet, 1840–43; new church at Shadwell, 1840–42; alterations to the Court House, Leeds, 1840–41; new church at Leven, 1840–45.
[118] ICBS, 1422 (Holmbridge); see below, pp. 103–04.

churches representing the full range of Romanesque and Gothic idioms, and his public buildings show an equally broad range of Classical and Tudor styles. His ability to advise on the latest technology, which he did in recommending a new heating system for the Court House; to design temporary buildings; and suggest effective remedies for outbreaks of dry-rot, illustrate the wide range of his professional services. Indeed, one might conclude that not only was he professionally successful, but that he was held in such high esteem as to be offered commissions in areas of architecture in which he had little or no previous experience.

From the late 1830s Chantrell had the assistance of two of his sons, John, born in 1815, and Henry, born in 1826. Throughout his career, Chantrell had had a series of pupils, but his sons must have been a useful addition to the office staff. Their first recorded work is in connection with the parish church at Leeds. R. W. Moore, Chantrell's pupil at this time, wrote,

> H. W. Chantrell (the architect's son) . . . was brought up an architect, and . . . was in his father's office along with myself and his brother John during the whole period of pulling down the old structure and rebuilding of the present edifice, and by and amongst whom most of the working drawings were made, and the execution of several parts superintended . . .[119]

However, it was John who, subsequently, seems to have played the more active part in the office. For the first time, in March 1840, the practice used the style Chantrell and Son[120] to refer to the partnership between R. D. and J. B. Chantrell. Following the completion of Leeds Parish Church, Henry, who was still only in his teens, spent 1842 and 1843 as clerk of works for the new church at Honley, near Huddersfield, and subsequently acted in that capacity at a number of other Chantrell churches.

In 1841, although the practice was busy with schemes started in earlier years, it seems only one new commission was started, the school attached to Christ Church, Leeds. The reason for this sudden change is likely to have been twofold; first, 1840 had probably been so hectic that Chantrell vowed never again to take so much work, and second, by the end of that year his financial position was such that he would no longer have needed to work so hard. Not only

[119] R. W. Moore, *A History of the Parish Church of Leeds* (Leeds, 1877), p. 54.
[120] This was in an advertisement for tenders for the new church at Batley Carr, *LI*, 28 March 1840.

had the recent success of the practice brought him substantial fees, but, on 12 May 1840, his father died, and as his eldest son Robert Dennis would presumably have come into a considerable inheritance.[121]

In 1842 R. D. Chantrell appears to take a further step back from professional practice with the appearance of the firm of Chantrell and Shaw, with J. B. Chantrell and Thomas Shaw as the two partners. Shaw had earlier been clerk of works for the rebuilding of the parish church. The first reference to the partnership comes in an advertisement in the *Leeds Intelligencer* of 25 June 1842, when tenders were requested for the building of a house at Headingley, and the address given for the firm is 6 Park Row. Between June 1842 and early in 1845, when the partnership was dissolved, Chantrell and Shaw were apparently responsible for new churches at Denholme Gate, Roberttown, Rise, Halifax and Keighley, as well as a school and a number of houses. The only new commission started by R. D. Chantrell in 1842 was a report on the roof of St John's, Golcar. He had been invited personally by the archdeacon to offer suggestions for curing a troublesome roof, after various architects had tried and failed, and the necessary work was carried out in 1843–44, not under his supervision, but under that of Chantrell and Shaw. It would seem that the beginning of 1843 saw him move another stage further from the demands of professional practice by giving up his office. R. W. Moore, Chantrell's former pupil, announced that he was setting himself up in the profession, with his office at '11 and 12, Benson's Building, or 2, Park Row, Leeds, lately occupied by R. D. Chantrell'.[122] From then until he left Leeds, Chantrell worked from his residence, *Oatlands*.[123]

His known commissions in 1843 consisted of the rebuilding of the Norman roof of Adel church, surveying the partly Norman church at East Ardsley, surveying Hunslet chapel for the proposed alterations, and designing a monument to 'Mrs Abbutt', carved by D. Wilson of Leeds, and erected in Dewsbury parish church. Also in 1843, work began on the new termination to the tower of Bruges Cathedral, which Chantrell had designed in 1839, with R. Buyck acting as executant architect. With the exception of Hunslet chapel,

---

[121] See above, p. 16–17.

[122] *LI*, 28 Jan. 1843.

[123] Messrs Horsfall and Harrison, Solicitors, who acted for the building committee of Leeds Parish Church, paid a number of professional visits to Chantrell at his house in 1844 and 1845 to discuss aspects of the building accounts (LPCA, 41/13). In Jan. 1846 Chantrell advertised land in Headingley which he had for sale, and gave his address for prospective purchasers as *Oatlands*.

it would seem that Chantrell had selected for himself the interesting work and passed on most of the 'new' work to his son and Shaw. The year 1844 produced a similar pattern; he prepared plans for a new church for East Ardsley, perhaps incorporating parts of the original building, and for an extension to Armley chapel. Meanwhile, Chantrell and Shaw began work on further new ecclesiastical and secular buildings. The last known commission to be started by them was the rebuilding of Keighley parish church in January 1845.

After the dissolution of the partnership between Chantrell and Shaw in February 1845, apparently as a result of Shaw's 'blunders',[124] Shaw quickly established a partnership with John Dobson. The *Intelligencer* of 22 February 1845 carried a notice of the dissolution of partnership and elsewhere in the same edition was an announcement of the formation of a partnership between Shaw and Dobson, with an office at 19 Park Row. Subsequently, R. D. and J. B. Chantrell worked together under the style of Messrs Chantrell, also with an office at 19 Park Row.[125] Following the separation of J. B. Chantrell and Shaw, the latter was given the completion of All Saints, Roberttown, near Huddersfield, but Messrs Chantrell supervised the remaining work on the other unfinished projects. Also, in 1845 and 1846 they began work on a further three new churches, those at Leeds (St Philip's), Middleton, near Leeds, and Armitage Bridge.

One important question remains about the last phase of Chantrell's career in Leeds: the extent of R. D. Chantrell's involvement in the work of Chantrell and Shaw, and subsequently Messrs Chantrell. It is the author's belief that R. D. Chantrell was responsible for all the important designs nominally produced by both of these partnerships, and that both partnerships existed to allow him to continue to produce designs without necessarily having to become involved in the tiresome day-to-day running of an office. Furthermore, they allowed him to spend time in London in the early and mid 1840s. Most importantly, these arrangements enabled him to devote time to the study of the 'Geometrical Principles in Gothic Architecture',[126] to the perfection of the theoretical model for the layout of buildings according to these principles, and to the subsequent experimentation with this in the design and erection of new churches. Indeed, all but one of the new churches which appeared as the work of either

[124] CBC, Halifax file, no. 16867. The *Intelligencer* of 22 Feb. 1845 carried a notice of the dissolution of the partnership.
[125] The first appearance of the new family partnership comes in the *Intelligencer* of 28 June 1845 when tenders are requested for the new church at Middleton.
[126] This is discussed in more detail on pp. 109–19.

partnership were subsequently claimed to have been designed by him according to his 'principle'. He gave additional details of his contribution to the partnership in a letter which he wrote to the Church Building Commissioners on 28 February 1845, explaining the dissolution of the Chantrell and Shaw partnership.

> In consequence of the several alterations made by Shaw and his setting all plans and specifications at nought (?), my son John has separated from him and I am examining all their works (as far as those which I entrusted to them) and rectifying the blunders committed by Shaw; I find the drawings . . . given by Shaw to the contractors for . . . Halifax . . . to be at variance with my original designs . . . I . . . have plans for Middleton Church nearly ready . . .[127]

Whether all the known work of Chantrell and Shaw was designed by R. D. Chantrell is not clear, but the letter quoted above suggests that they had in progress some works which he had not 'entrusted to them'. In this category could be a number of houses for which Chantrell and Shaw advertised requests for tenders.[128] Letters to the architectural press[129] show that the new churches of Messrs Chantrell were also designed by R. D. Chantrell, and from the period of this partnership are apparently independent works by R. D. Chantrell. For instance, the chancel of the thirteenth- and fourteenth-century church at Lund in the East Riding was rebuilt in 1845–46 and the architect is recorded as R. D. Chantrell rather than Messrs Chantrell. Nevertheless, increasingly through the 1840s, Chantrell was not only withdrawing from the practice of architecture, but was also spending time away from Leeds. He maintained his membership of the Philosophical and Literary Society until 1846, but after 1843 there is no known record of his having taken part in any activity in the town, or offering any contribution to its public affairs.

At the beginning of 1847 Chantrell announced his removal to London although a number of building projects remained unfinished; Messrs Chantrell continued to have an office in Leeds until at least 1851.[130]

[127] CBC, Halifax file.
[128] For example, *LI*, 25 June 1842 and 23 July 1842.
[129] *Civil Engineer and Architect's Journal*, April 1846, p.100; and *Builder*, V (1847), p.302.
[130] W. Slade, *Slade and Roebuck's Directory of the Borough and Neighbourhood of Leeds* (Leeds, 1851), p.182 includes 'Chantrell and Son, Architects, 12, Park Row'. There is no mention of the practice in the next relevant directory, which was published in 1853.

CHAPTER 4

Ecclesiastical Commissions

Ecclesiastical commissions proved to be the backbone of Chantrell's career; he received at least fifty appointments to build or alter Anglican churches and chapels. Certainly his modest significance in the context of English architecture of the first half of the nineteenth century lies in his Gothic churches rather than his Classical secular works. However, it is instructive to set this achievement against his inauspicious start as a designer of churches. Before and during Chantrell's period of pupilage, Soane received no significant ecclesiastical commissions. Furthermore, his lectures and the programme of study he set his pupils make it clear he had little interest in Gothic as an architectural style. In the comprehensive records of Chantrell's apprenticeship there is no explicit statement that he spent any time studying the churches of the middle ages. It is hardly surprising, therefore, that when, towards the end of his career, Chantrell looked back to his early ecclesiastical commissions, he admitted that he had 'worked without system – merely adopting features to masses to which [he] could give no just proportion'.[1] He explained that he and the other architects employed in the erection of Gothic churches

> though generally well grounded in Greek and Roman architecture, found themselves called upon to construct works utterly at variance with Greek and Roman principles; and having no time to study or collect data, whereon to compose works in this (to them) new style, they were required at once to erect buildings equally at variance with its principles, in which the greatest number of sittings could be crowded into the smallest area, and adapt the fragments of the various medieval styles to their utilitarian masses . . .[2]

[1] *Builder*, V (1847), p.300. C. R. Cockerell, an architect of Chantrell's generation, in a lecture to the Royal Academy in 1846 expressed a similar view: '[I] had always greatly admired the [Gothic] style but we merely copied the forms and did not possess the principles . . .', quoted in D. Watkin, *The Life and Work of C. R. Cockerell* (1974), p.127.
[2] *Builder*, V (1847), p.300.

Why then was Chantrell so consistent in his use of a style which he found so difficult to adopt? The answer is surely for expediency. Indeed, he believed that the 1818 Church Building Act was 'a firm opportunity for restoring the best examples of Greece and Rome'.[3] However, Chantrell perceived that Leeds and the neighbouring towns had 'submitted to the county mania for plain Gothic works . . . I should wish to present a Grecian or Roman design, but the objections to them made by local committees would be so strong that I fear my labour would be entirely lost . . .'.[4] He was probably quite correct in this assumption since ninety-eight of the ninety-nine churches subsequently erected in the West Riding of Yorkshire by the Church Building Commission between 1821 and 1856 were 'Gothic'.[5] Thomas Taylor had already established the precedent that new churches should be in this style through a number of accomplished designs, for instance at Christ Church, Liversedge (1812–16) and St Lawrence, Pudsey (1821–24), which had, according to Chantrell, 'given great satisfaction to the Archbishop of York and other exalted ecclesiastics'.[6] Chantrell thus found himself in a situation where, following the passing of the 1818 Church Building Act, there were opportunities to secure important commissions if he could adapt his skills of architectural composition to this unfamiliar style.

Ecclesiastical commissions were to take Chantrell on a number of occasions into Cheshire, Derbyshire and the East Riding. However his development as a designer of churches can be studied effectively in relation to examples in, or near to, Leeds. For convenience, these examples which make up the remainder of this chapter, are divided into five periods.

1819–1826

In all probability, Chantrell's first attempt at securing a commission for a Gothic church was in *c.*1820. In a letter of January 1821 he wrote: 'I was lately introduced by Mr Gott . . . to Sir James Graham

[3] SM, Private Correspondence, xv, A, 32: Chantrell to Soane, 6 Jan. 1821.
[4] *Ibid.*, Chantrell believed it was the clergy who, 'where they had sufficient influence, induced local committees to adopt [Gothic] for their new churches': *Builder*, V (1847), p.300. His 'fears' were borne out by C. R. Cockerell who, in 1822, submitted a Classical design for a chapel for Lord Middleton at Birdsall in Yorkshire. It was rejected in favour of a Gothic design by Hodgson Fowler: Watkin, p.250.
[5] Here 'Gothic' includes Norman. The one exception is St James's, Wakefield, by S. Sharp, 1829–30, which is Classical.
[6] SM, Private Correspondence, xv, A, 32.

D

for whom I have designed a small church proposed to be erected on his property near Kirkstall Abbey . . .'.[7] This is the sole known reference to Graham's intention to build a church at this date and there is no reason for thinking that the scheme developed any further at this time. However, Chantrell's St Stephen's, Kirkstall, built at the end of the decade, was perhaps the end result of the 1820 proposal.

Chantrell's first three executed Gothic designs were Christ Church, Leeds, and alteration to the chapels at Armley and Bramley. The precise chronological sequence of these designs is not clear although they belong to the period 1821–25. While Christ Church is certainly the major commission of the trio, it can be understood best in the context of the lesser two which will be discussed first.

Over a twelve year period Chantrell did a variety of work at Bramley Chapel beginning in 1821. In October of that year he was paid for 'taking down the old belfry . . . designing a new belfry and erecting it'.[8] However, by the following year this had become structurally unsound and on 16 August 1822 an appeal for financial assistance was made to the Society for Promoting the Enlargement, Building and Repairing of Churches and Chapels. This stated the congregation's desire to build a new church, 65 feet by 42 feet to hold 800, on new ground using the old materials at cost, estimated by Chantrell, of £1,870. As a less satisfactory alternative he suggested an addition, the whole length of the south from 10 feet 6 inches wide and a small east chancel with a tower over it.[9] Both proposals were rejected by the Society as funds were not available, and presumably some repairs must have been made, as the turret stayed in place until 1833 when Chantrell extended the chapel.[10] The drawing of Chantrell's 1822 scheme for extending the church suggests that at this stage in his career he did indeed 'work without a system' on these compositions. It is not an unattractive scheme but it would seem to demonstrate that the author had little understanding or knowledge of either the principles or details of medieval architecture (Plate 11(a)).

The following year, Chantrell was engaged in proposed extensions to Armley chapel.[11] a building of about 1630[12] designed in a crude

[7] *Ibid*.

[8] A. Dobson, *St Peter's Church at Bramley* (Leeds, 1964), p.31.

[9] ICBS, 413 (Bramley).

[10] *Ibid*. and A. Dobson, p.33.

[11] It is difficult to give a date for the work but it seems likely that Chantrell's first proposal came in 1823 and this was carried out, in a slightly modified form, in 1825.

[12] Taylor, p.100.

Perpendicular style. By the 1820s more accommodation was needed and, in particular, Benjamin Gott required additional pews for his family and servants. Chantrell proposed an addition on the north side of the chancel which in form and detail merely reproduced the mediocre seventeenth-century work; he made no attempt at an original composition (Plate 12(a)).

Leeds was relatively slow in applying to the Commissioners for money to build new churches, but on 10 June 1820 the *Intelligencer* was able to announce: 'His Majesty's Commissioners . . . deem it expedient that three new churches be built in the Parish [of Leeds], each capable of accommodating 1,200 persons with the capability of further accommodation should the population require it . . . The situations fixed upon are, one at Meadow Lane, one upon Quarry Hill and one between Woodhouse and Woodhouse Carr . . .'. Chantrell's appointment as architect for the church intended for Meadow Lane was announced in the *Intelligencer* of 14 May 1821, but the foundation stone was not laid until 29 January 1823;[13] the church was consecrated on 12 January 1826[14] as Christ Church (Plate 11(b)). This was a major commission for Chantrell: the final cost of the building – £10,555 – made it his most expensive undertaking so far; until he began work on the rebuilding of Leeds Parish Church in 1837, the budgets for his churches were less than one-third of this sum. The finished building had a commanding presence, its massive and richly decorated tower dominating the south side of the town. The Christ Church commission was a major one for Chantrell, not only from the point of view of the budget but, most importantly, because it represented the beginning of a long and fruitful relationship between Chantrell and the Commissioners who administered the post-1818 church-building programme, and led to his specializing in ecclesiastical commissions.

Chantrell's work at Bramley and Armley serves as a useful context in which to examine Christ Church. It is difficult to date the latter design, although early 1821 is probable. This would mean that it ante-dated the proposed extension to Bramley by about one year, and the enlargement of Armley by several years. Even if the Christ Church design took on its final form only just before building work commenced, the scheme is still concurrent with Bramley and earlier than Armley. The chronological sequence of the three designs is perplexing. There are affinities between Bramley and Armley but not between these two and Christ Church. The difference is

[13] *LI*, 30 Jan. 1823.
[14] LCA, Christ Church Parish Papers, no. 54.

essentially that the Christ Church design is much more sophisticated, suggesting it was later and not earlier than the other two. For instance, if a comparison is made between the proposed east elevation of Bramley (Plate 11(a)) with the west elevation of Christ Church (Plate 11(b)) this point becomes clearer. Both schemes are of three bays and are symmetrical, both use battlements and pinnacles, both have a tower in which the ascending stages are reduced in area, and the clock surrounds are similar. However, the whole character of the designs is different: Bramley is essentially two dimensional, whereas Christ Church explores fully the possibilities of the third dimension, which is so important for a successful Gothic design. It is not easy to explain convincingly how designs as naïve and unimaginative as Bramley and Armley could have post-dated the skilfully arranged and coherent Christ Church scheme. One answer is that Chantrell did not in fact design Christ Church. The London architect Francis Goodwin had initially been very successful in securing work from the Commissioners, so much so that they questioned his ability to manage all the schemes he had in hand and resolved that he should receive no more for the time being. In an attempt to overcome this restriction Goodwin induced other architects to offer his designs as their own on condition that the fee would be divided between them. There is sound evidence for thinking that Goodwin attempted to secure the Quarry Hill commission in this way using Charles Busby as his intermediary,[15] and may have had dealings of this type with Chantrell over Christ Church. It is undeniable that the west front of Christ Church bears many similarities to Goodwin's/Busby's designs of this period (Plate 12(b)) and none at all to Chantrell's. Alternatively, perhaps the 'Local Committee' in Leeds asked Chantrell to plagiarize the Goodwin design, or at least to modify his west elevation to incorporate the principal features of a Goodwin scheme. Fortunately, no hint of this reached the *Intelligencer's* readers; as far as the citizens of Leeds were concerned this was Chantrell's design and he was congratulated for it. Furthermore, it seems to have been regarded as the most successful of the three Commissioner's churches of the mid 1820s.[16] Never again did Chantrell specify the rich ornament of Christ Church in his designs – probably because he was never given

---

[15] See Webster, pp.172–78. The dispute which followed the rejection of Busby's design is fully documented in the following: M. H. Port, 'Francis Goodwin, 1784–1853', *Architectural History*, I (1958), pp.60–72; *Monthly Magazine*, iv (1822), pp.211–12; Busby published a pamphlet defending his designs, a copy of which is in the Victoria and Albert Museum Library, Box I 35J.

[16] J. Heaton, *A Walk Through Leeds*, pp.104–07.

such a generous budget, but the plan was one which, with very little variation, he used in all his new churches for the next ten years.

1826–1831

Despite the doubts which might be raised concerning the authorship of the Christ Church design, the board of the Church Building Commission must have been well pleased with it as, in the five years (1826–31) which followed its completion, Chantrell was responsible for a further six new churches for it.[17] These were: St George's, New Mills, Derbyshire; Emmanuel, Lockwood, near Huddersfield (Plate 13(a)); St Peter's, Morley (Plates 14(a) and (b)); St Stephen's, Kirkstall, Leeds (Plate 13(b)); All Saints, Netherthong, near Huddersfield; and St Matthew's, Holbeck, Leeds (Plate 15(a)). These, together with submitted but unexecuted designs for new churches at Bramley, Hyde (Cheshire) and Horwich (Lancashire), plus simultaneous enlargements and restorations of other churches, indicate a prolific period in Chantrell's career as a church architect.

Although the six completed churches were all built with the aid of the Parliamentary Church Building Commission, they were erected at considerably less cost than the earlier Christ Church, Leeds. The latter had been financed from the first parliamentary grant when, despite the limited funds, large, impressive churches were required and at a cost, in the north of England, of about £6 to £7 per sitting. The churches of the late 1820s onwards belong to the era of the second parliamentary grant, when the need for economy was even more pressing. Reductions in size and ornamentation produced significant savings and the cost per sitting was about half that of the 'first grant' churches. These six new churches can be placed stylistically in one of two groups. The smaller ones at Lockwood and Netherthong form the first group and those at Holbeck, Morley, Kirkstall and New Mills, with rather more accommodation, make up the second. Although the building of these six churches was more or less concurrent, the designs for Lockwood and Netherthong, which belong to around September 1826, are slightly earlier than those for the other four churches which belong to 1827–28. The New Mills design can be dated to around June or July 1827, that for Kirkstall to about July to November 1827, while the Morley scheme belongs to March to May 1828 and that for Holbeck to about the same period.

[17] This was the maximum number of churches which the Commissioners believed an architect should be engaged on at any one time.

Although there is less than twelve months between the designs of
the two groups of churches, they nevertheless indicate a distinct
change in Chantrell's approach to the Gothic style. While Lockwood
and Netherthong in some ways look back to Bramley and Christ
Church, the other group was more forward looking[18] and represents
a more 'correct' and sophisticated series of solutions to the problems
imposed by designing what was essentially a 'modern' type of
building but one which was required to have a cheap veneer of
medievalism.

The churches of the second group all display the same basic
pattern but each is different in detail, with its own characteristics.
They are not only bigger than those of the first group but all have
towers and spires[19] instead of bellcotes. More importantly, the
churches of the second group suggest that Chantrell was trying to
capture the spirit of medieval architecture; he was not so much
concerned with applying relatively small-scale Gothic elements to
his modern 'box', as trying to achieve a total mass and contour
reminiscent of the middle ages, made up of units as big as a whole
elevation, discriminatingly taken from a specific medieval structure.
In July 1827, when Chantrell submitted his designs for New Mills
(the earliest church in the second group), his accompanying letter
stated, 'I hope this style, which is a collection from some specimens
of the 13th century, will meet with [the Board's] approbation'.[20]
Even more interesting and indicative of Chantrell's increased concern
with archaeology is a letter which he wrote to the Board in
September 1828 describing his design for Hyde church: 'I have in
progress a design in the Early English style (Henry III) partly on a
model as far as respects the west front of Ripon Minster and the east
part a composition from buildings of the same date which abound
in this county . . .'.[21]

The churches of the second group are all cheaper in terms of cost
per sitting than Lockwood and Netherthong. Furthermore, the cost
of towers and spires for this group, which was not incurred by the

---

[18] For instance, towers similar to the ones specified for these four can be found in
Chantrell's work of 20 years later.

[19] The spire of Holbeck, although part of the original design, was not built until
1860: Taylor, p. 376.

[20] CBC MB 26, p. 234.

[21] CBC MB 32, pp. 301–2. This design although subsequently rejected by the
Commissioners, is notable in that it contained two west towers. Such a specification
was highly unusual at this time although not unique; Chantrell's design was
produced at about the same time as the completion of the National Scotch Church
in Sidmouth Street, London, designed by William Tite. In this church the west
front is based loosely on York Minster.

first group, must have reduced still further the amount of money available for the body of the church and its decoration. Thus Chantrell turned from the expensive Decorated style of the first group to the much cheaper Early English. In the Holbeck design he was urged to make stringent economies[22] and in accompaniment with the plans sent to the Board he wrote: 'In the design I have adhered to the style of the early part of the reign of Henry III which is the most economical that can be adopted and it possesses a degree of elegant simplicity rarely found in decorative examples of the 14th century as far as respects the contour'.[23] Of his design for New Mills he wrote, '. . . it is substantial and economical . . .'.[24]

In plan, the four churches of the second group are almost identical. The seven-bay rectangular body of the church has projections at the east and west ends for chancel and tower respectively. The spaces left in the corners by these projections were filled with staircases or vestries, and these were given lower roofs to add visual interest to the buildings. A more detailed examination of Morley, which is typical of this group, suggests some of the sources that Chantrell was using at this time (Plates 14(a) and (b)). Morley was designed only a few months before the rejected Hyde scheme and it seems that Ripon Cathedral also influenced Morley although in a less obvious way. At Morley the single, central, west tower shares a number of details with either of those at Ripon and the spire is typical of those of the thirteenth century. In particular, it could have been based on that at All Saints, Glossop, which Chantrell had surveyed recently. The east end, with three lancet windows under a continuous moulding, might have been developed from the north transept of Rievaulx Abbey or the east end of Whitby Abbey. The plain north and south sides, with their straight lines of windows, could have been derived from parts of Kirkstall Abbey or Fountains.

The interiors of all of the three Leeds churches have been altered detrimentally. However, New Mills, which is reasonably well preserved, is not unattractive. In particular it does not seem so 'barn-like' as those churches in the group which have lost their side galleries. In their original states, all four had low pitched roofs spanning the entire width of the body of the church with no division into nave and aisles. They had galleries on three sides supported by

---

[22] His initial estimate was for £4,950 (CBC MB 25, p.244). A little later this was reduced to £4,000 (CBC MB 26, p.131) then to £3,500 (CBC MB 37, p.299) although the actual cost was £3,734 18s. 4½d.

[23] CBC MB 32, pp.300–1.

[24] CBC MB 26, p.234.

thin cast-iron columns and a wide arch in the east wall opening into a shallow chancel.

1831–1838

The second parliamentary grant of 1824, which was wholly or principally responsible for financing Chantrell's six churches of the late 1820s, was almost exhausted by 1830, and the Commissioners' influence waned with their funds. After his appointment to design Morley church (1828), it was fifteen years before Chantrell was again required to erect a new church built with their aid. It was not for some years that private munificence was available on a scale which enabled lavish church building projects to be undertaken without the assistance of a grant. Consequently, in the 1830s the repair and economical extension of decaying and undersized buildings was the only course available to many parishes in order to extend their church accommodation. Of the six new churches which Chantrell began in the late 1820s, Holbeck, consecrated in December 1831, was the last to be finished. He was then obliged to undertake the less prestigious, although not always uninteresting, tasks of low budget improvements to existing churches. One such commission was at Glossop and this usefully puts into context several of Chantrell's appointments of the 1830s. All Saints, Glossop, was a basically medieval building which, only five years before Chantrell was asked to survey it, had been partially rebuilt at a cost of over £1,000 by Edward Drury, a Sheffield architect. Already the walls were bulging badly. However, Chantrell soon identified the problem and during 1831–32 rebuilt large parts of the church. The finished building was unremarkable and not especially attractive, but, more importantly for the parishioners, Chantrell's repairs were effective and relatively cheap.[25] It was these qualities of structural dependability coupled with economy that churchwardens required in their buildings once it was they who paid the bills[26] rather than the Commissioners in London. Unreliable, and often needlessly expensive builder/architects like Drury were numerous in the provinces; professional architects, who could repair economically the effects of years of neglect and often poor workmanship in the first place, and in even the cheapest restorations could produce a building whose new appearance was in keeping with the recently

[25] ICBS, 456 (Glossop).
[26] It is true that in many cases the ICBS made a contribution but the parish invariably had to pay the major part of the cost.

heightened standards of decency in church architecture, were bound to be in demand. Such skills could not easily be found and Chantrell was to benefit from the paucity of competition for these commissions.

In October 1830 the churchwardens of Guiseley resolved 'that Mr Chantrell be instructed to give an estimate for repairing the church at Guiseley'.[27] Chantrell drew up the necessary plans in 1831 and work was carried out in 1832–33. The initial scheme had been little more than a rearrangement of the pews, but in July 1832 the north wall was pronounced by Chantrell to be badly inclined. He then proposed 'renewing [the church] in a more commodious plan, occupying the centre aisle with pews, widening the church, erecting a gallery on the north side, rebuilding the north wall and other repairs'.[28] Chantrell, who was described by the vicar as 'the architect whom we had so highly recommended to us',[29] estimated the total cost to be £998.[30]

While Glossop was a church that had been seriously mutilated by post-reformation alterations, St Oswald's, Guiseley, although dilapidated, possessed an impressive array of Norman and Gothic features,[31] and Chantrell's design for the outside of the new north aisle used elements of the Perpendicular tower – for example, diagonal buttresses terminating in elaborate pinnacles at the corners, and a moulded band running at the bottom of the window sills, which copied that at the bottom of the bell chamber openings. To what extent Chantrell's scheme was adopted is hard to ascertain and it is likely that he only rearranged the interior. More importantly, buildings like Guiseley extended his experience of medieval buildings. This experience was, subsequently, to prove most useful in the designing of new churches as well as in the repairing of old ones.

All Saints, Pontefract, which Chantrell restored in the early 1830s, was an even more interesting building. It was probably built between the thirteenth and fifteenth centuries and had a cruciform plan. Over the crossing was an unusual square tower terminating in an octagonal lantern. The church was badly damaged in the Civil War during one of the sieges of the nearby castle, and was largely left as a ruin.

[27] LCA, P29/III: Guiseley Overseers and Churchwardens Accounts, 1710–1833.
[28] ICBS, 1472 (Guiseley).
[29] Ibid.
[30] Ibid.
[31] Pevsner refers to it as 'One of the most interesting churches in this part of the West Riding'. It possesses a late Norman south doorway, a Norman south arcade, a 13th century transept and a Perpendicular tower: N. Pevsner, The Buildings of England: Yorkshire, The West Riding (1959), p.227.

Probably in 1831,[32] Chantrell was asked to supervise the creation of a small church within these remains (Plate 16(a)). Thus, for example, Chantrell quickly established himself as an expert in the restoration of medieval churches and, by implication, as an antiquarian. Thus Norrison Scatchard, the Morley antiquary, sought Chantrell's support when trying to secure the restoration of medieval wall paintings at St Mary's, Woodkirk, in 1831.[33]

Beginning in 1833, Chantrell was involved in further commissions at Armley and Bramley, two chapels on which he had worked in the 1820s. In both cases architecturally uninteresting and unpromising buildings were enlarged within a modest budget. Probably in 1825, Chantrell had designed a new chancel aisle and vestry at Armley in a project initiated by Benjamin Gott. In 1833 Gott again asked Chantrell to extend and repair the chapel which had become 'dilapidated owing to the north and south walls being badly built and graves been excavated below the foundations'.[34] Chantrell's proposals of 16 May 1833[35] were complicated although cheap and practical. One can see from the following that a commission of this type required considerable care in the planning stage and, no doubt, rigorous supervision during its execution. The schedule of work is complicated but, like Guiseley, it amply demonstrates Chantrell's ingenuity. The extension involved building a new north wall 13 feet out from the old one almost to double the area of the north aisle. The four plain iron columns which divided the nave and north aisle were to be replaced by ones in the same material, but in the Gothic style, and the position of the new columns was to be 3 feet 6 inches south of the old ones, to bring them in line with the original north wall of the chancel. The west wall was to be taken down and rebuilt incorporating a centrally placed small tower and including a copy of the west window of the nave at the west end of the new north aisle giving an overall balance to the west end. The new walls were to be 14 feet higher than the old ones, nearly doubling the height, and an 'L' shaped gallery, containing 261 sittings, was to be erected along the north and west walls. Subsequently, the roof of the nave was to be removed and placed on the widened north aisle, which by then would have assumed almost exactly the same dimensions as the nave. The south

---

[32] ICBS, 1347 (Pontefract): vicar of Pontefract to ICBS, 16 April 1831 stating that Chantrell had already produced the plans.
[33] Taylor, pp. 120–21; Webster, pp. 233–34.
[34] ICBS, 256 (Armley): application to ICBS for a grant, signed Benjamin Gott, 24 May 1833.
[35] ICBS, 256 (Armley).

wall was to be taken down and rebuilt in the same position, but to a higher level, and with a regularised arrangement of five pointed windows corresponding in position to the windows of the north wall, and the line of columns dividing nave and aisle. Finally, a new roof was to be placed over the nave. Chantrell's estimated cost was £1,030 and the work was expected to take three months. It was finished by November 1834 (Plate 15(b)).[36]

The chapel at Bramley probably dated from the seventeenth century, and was a plain rectangular structure which included a schoolroom at the 'west' end. The east window was pointed, but all the other windows were flat-headed and divided into strips by two mullions. The general character of the building was not unlike that of Armley Chapel. An 'L' shaped gallery, which ran along the west and north walls, was erected in 1813, facing the pulpit which was in the centre of the south wall. The downstairs pews inconveniently faced east, many of them having their backs to the pulpit. The churchwardens of Bramley tried unsuccessfully to finance the building of a new church in the 1820s. Thus on 2 April 1833 a committee was formed to carry out an enlargement of the existing chapel.[37] Bearing the same date is a pair of drawings by Chantrell proposing opening up the south side of the church to form a transept containing an organ gallery on the first floor (Plate 16(b)).[38]

The chapel was reopened on 27 October 1833;[39] the total cost of the renovations was £582 11s. 0d.[40] The new transept provided an extra 150 sittings and a more suitable place for the organ. The old organ gallery was taken down 'from which circumstances the east window has again been thrown open',[41] and the exterior was also improved. On the east and west sides of the 'transept' Chantrell placed rectangular windows which corresponded to those already existing in the chapel. He might even have reused some of the old windows from the demolished part of the south wall. However, on the south face of the transept, he produced a quite different style to give the building an appropriate ecclesiastical appearance. The 1821 cupola was reused in an elongated form; it was placed at the apex of the gable, and crowned by a new, taller spire.

[36] LI, 8 Nov. 1834.
[37] LCA, P14/144, Bramley Parish Records.
[38] ICBS, 413 (Bramley).
[39] LI, 26 Oct. 1833.
[40] ICBS, 413 (Bramley).
[41] LI, 2 Nov. 1833.

PLATE 17 (a)   SKIPTON: CHRIST CHURCH, 1835–39.

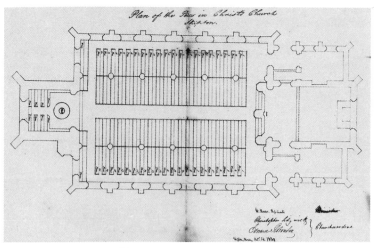

PLATE 17 (b)   SKIPTON: CHRIST CHURCH, 1835–39.
Plan 1839, probably not by Chantrell.

PLATE 18 (a)   HEADINGLEY, LEEDS: ST MICHAEL, 1836–38.
Watercolour by J. Rhodes.

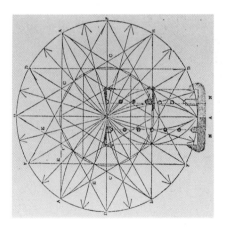

PLATE 18 (b)   CHANTRELL'S 'SYSTEM'.
Showing what he believed to be the system of proportions used by medieval masons
in designing their cathedrals and large churches.

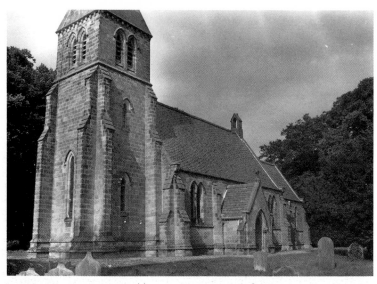

PLATE 19 (a)   RISE, ER: ALL SAINTS, 1844–45

PLATE 19 (b)   ROBERTTOWN, WR: ALL SAINTS, 1843–45.
Drawing possibly by Chantrell.

PLATE 20 (a)   ADEL, LEEDS: ST JOHN THE BAPTIST.
Photograph showing the west gable and bellcote built to Chantrell's designs in
1838–39.

PLATE 20 (b)   SHADWELL, LEEDS: ST PAUL, 1840–42.

PLATE 21 (b)   BRUGES, BELGIUM: CATHEDRAL OF
ST SAVIOUR.
Drawing by Chantrell showing proposed
additions to the tower, 1839.

PLATE 21 (a)   HONLEY, WR: ST MARY, 1840–44.

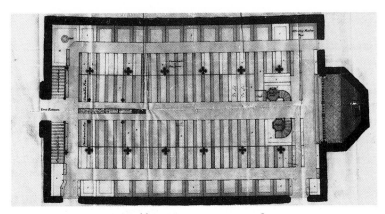

PLATE 22 (a)   HONLEY, WR: ST MARY 1840–44.
Plans drawn by W. H. Chantrell, 1844.

PLATE 22 (b)   MIDDLETON, LEEDS: ST MARY, 1845–46.
Lithograph, based on a drawing by Chantrell, showing the church from the south
west. The top half of the lithograph is missing.

PLATE 23 (a)   KING CROSS, HALIFAX: ST PAUL, 1844–47.
Lithograph by J. K. Coling.

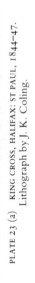

PLATE 23 (b)   LEEDS: ST PHILIP, 1845–47.
Lithograph by Pulleyn and Hunt.

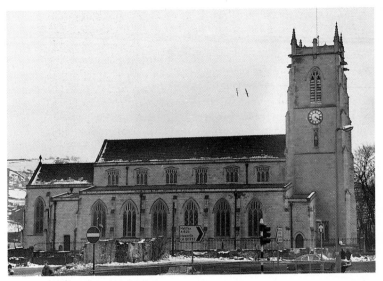

PLATE 24 (a)   KEIGHLEY: ST ANDREW, 1845–48.

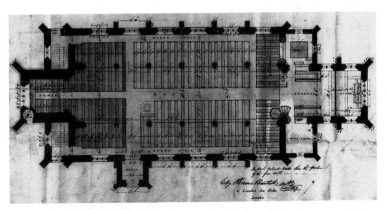

PLATE 24 (b)   KEIGHLEY: ST ANDREW, 1845–48, PLAN.
Drawing by Chantrell, 1849.

In contrast to the new work at Guiseley and Pontefract that at Armley and Bramley might be thought of as crude and lacking 'correctness'. However, it is probably fairer to assume that Chantrell followed the character of the existing buildings and, at Armley and Bramley, avoided the temptation of inappropriate medievalism.

The ancient churches at Glossop, Guiseley and Pontefract enabled Chantrell to gain invaluable first-hand knowledge of Gothic forms and details. Clearly it was through this sort of experience that subsequently he developed into an expert on that style. His skills in decoration were complemented by the experience acquired while planning his most important commission of the mid 1830s, a new church at Skipton (Plates 17(a) and (b)). Although this commission falls outside the main geographical area of this study, it deserves mention. The real significance of the appointment is that it introduced Chantrell to Daniel Parsons and Christopher Sidgewick who were to become perpetual curate and churchwarden respectively. Parsons wished to build 'a true Christian edifice'[42] and Sidgewick, who supervised the interior arrangements, wished 'to make it precisely conformable to what was designed by the Reformers of the Church of England, and to render it easy for the officiating minister to observe its Rubrics to the strictness of the letter . . .'.[43] The result was a church quite unlike anything already designed by Chantrell in plan or elevation. Indeed, at the time, it was one of the country's most 'advanced' ecclesiastical buildings. There is a long chancel raised above the nave by steps, a nave with clerestory, and side aisles. The church should be seen in a wider context than Chantrell's career and its place in the history of the Gothic Revival and Ecclesiology deserves more attention. It would be interesting to know what the Camden Society and the participants in the Oxford Movement would have made of it, for it seems to incorporate all their primary objectives yet pre-dates their movement by several years and, if the executed design of Christ Church, Skipton, was conceived in 1834–35, it anticipates the publications of Pugin. It enabled Chantrell to be among the country's first architects to understand the architectural implications of the movement within the Church of England for greater emphasis on ritual in its worship. When, in the 1840s, this movement gathered momentum, he was well placed to give an architectural lead.

Such advanced thinking about church arrangements and liturgy must have needed time to be fully assimilated and perhaps it was

[42] ICBS, 2047 (Skipton).
[43] *Gentleman's Magazine*, 176, (1839), p. 532.

only when these ideas were reinforced by Walter Farquhar Hook[44] during the rebuilding of St Peter's, Leeds, that Chantrell really began to appreciate their significance. Thus Chantrell's design for the new church of St Michael at Headingley, built during the same period as Skipton, although unusual, seems not to have been influenced by the views of Parsons and Sidgewick.

The old chapel at Headingley was over 200 years old and contained seats for only 207 people. It was so dilapidated that an enlargement, as opposed to rebuilding, seemed out of the question. Accordingly, on 19 December 1836 the faculty for rebuilding was applied for.[45] The finished building consisted of a nave, a deep chancel, transepts, a western tower, a south porch and a canted projection on the north side of the nave to accommodate the gallery stairs (Plate 18(a)). While it would be tempting to see this as a further example of Chantrell's growing interest in medieval church planning, his drawings show that the chancel was to contain four large 'box' pews with only a very restricted amount of space around the altar. The positions of old foundations do not provide a convincing explanation for the shape of the new building. Perhaps the 'transept' which Chantrell had added at Bramley might have been the model for those at Headingley, and reminded him that this was a practical and economical way of producing a significant increase of space. Certainly the new plan for Headingley provided a very compact arrangement of large box pews grouped around the 'three decker' pulpit, with the smaller pews and free seats further away, but with none of them too far distant from the pulpit. The whole building was erected for the very modest sum of £2,581[46] and was opened on 31 January 1838.[47]

In March 1837 Chantrell began to prepare designs for a new church at Holmbridge, south of Huddersfield. Eventually these were rejected, but the surviving documentation illustrates what was involved in the planning stage of a typical commission, and it gives an insight into professional practice in this period. Chntrell's account listed:

| 1837 | March | 25 | For the design of a church to hold 500 on the ground floor, according to instructions given. |
| | April | 2 | A fair copy of the plan. |

[44] It is of interest, perhaps, that Hook was present at the opening of Skipton church.
[45] LCA, P39/84, Headingley Parish Records.
[46] Ibid.
[47] LI, 3 February 1838.

		10	Making (?) drawings and calculating sittings.
May		1	Copies of plans of Ground and Gallery floors with sections, and calculating sittings
		2	Making estimates of the cost of the building.
		3–6	Clerk's time making out copies.
		9–19	Making working drawings and details for the Incorporated Society.
		31	Completion of drawings.
June		6–13	Specifications and copies thereof.
July		17	Attending Incorporated Society in London respecting the drawings.
August		8	Attending Incorporated Society in London when returning from the Continent.
December		4	At Armitage Bridge taking instructions of new (?) alterations to suit the Society.
		6	Made out another plan and copy.
1838	January	8	Made plan of ground floor, description and alterations.
		9	Another plan, altering sittings, placing free seats in the middle aisle, and copy.

He calculated the time spent as twenty-one days' work, and charged for his time at 2 guineas per day, making a total of £44 2s. 0d.[48]

1838–1842

Chantrell began work on rebuilding Leeds Parish Church in 1837 (Plates 25(a)–29(b)) and almost immediately a significant number of other ecclesiastical commissions followed. This group of church commissions occupy the period of the rebuilding of the parish church and the early 1840s. During this time he designed new churches at Lothersdale and Cowling (both near Skipton), at Farnley Tyas and Honley (both near Huddersfield) (Plates 21(a) and 22(a)), and at Batley and at Leven (E. Riding). Simultaneously he was involved with the restoration of Bruges Cathedral. In the Leeds area he built only two very small churches, St Wilfrid's, Pool, and St Paul's, Shadwell (Plate 20(b)), but repaired or altered a number of others. These included Holy Trinity, where he added a new upper section to the storm damaged eighteenth-century tower, and

[48] ICBS, 1422 (Holmbridge).

demonstrated that he had lost none of his ability to design successfully in the Classical style (Plates 9(a) and (b)). Two of the commissions arose as a direct result of the closure of the parish church for reconstruction: a small brick oratory was built in 1838 in the New Church Yard, so that some services could take place there while the parish church was closed;[49] however, most of the services were transferred to St John's where Chantrell supervised the construction of additional galleries as well as other alterations.[50]

Chantrell's professional success in this period can be seen to result from an interaction of three factors: the Leeds Parish Church commission which significantly enhanced his professional reputation in Yorkshire; his unusually good knowledge of medieval architecture acquired after twenty years in practice; his understanding of construction which could be relied upon to produce sound buildings. It is instructive to examine these three, often overlapping, areas in more detail.

From his contact with Sidgewick at Skipton and, more importantly, Hook in Leeds, Chantrell was well acquainted with the latest developments in Anglican worship. That Chantrell's reputation was decidedly low in the estimation of the writers in the *Ecclesiologist* is misleading. It is, perhaps, useful to see those who contributed to the developments in Anglican worship and its setting as belonging to two categories. First, there were the theorists: those belonging to the Oxford Movement and, slightly later, the members of the Cambridge Camden Society. Second, there were those, usually less well known, figures who were instrumental in building churches, using whatever financial and academic resources were available, yet aiming for something better than a 'Commissioners' preaching box'. It seems logical that such a distinction should be made. Basil Clarke and J. F. White have pointed out[51] that, initially, the leaders of the Oxford Movement did not play a prominent role in the revival of Gothic architecture. The Ecclesiologists were quite clear about the need to unite ritual and architecture, yet avoided the responsibility of producing specific designs for achieving this. Chantrell saw the architect's role quite clearly. In a paper read to the Institute of British Architects in 1847,[52] in which he reviewed the 'great improvements' of the previous five or six years, he said: 'It is indispensable that

---

[49] LPCA, no.41/7: Building Committee Minute Book; no.41/5: Building Committee Accounts Book.

[50] LPCA, no.41/5: Building Committee Accounts Book.

[51] B. F. L. Clarke, *Church Builders of the Nineteenth Century* (Newton Abbot, 1969), pp.45–46, and J. F. White, *The Cambridge Movement* (Oxford, 1979), pp.16–24.

[52] *Ecclesiologist*, VIII (1848), p.132.

architects should not only keep pace with the clerical members of the local Architectural Societies but be foremost in all antiquarian researches, and enquiries relative to the methods employed by our forefathers, and the reasons by which they were guided, in the construction of the numerous beautiful and harmonious works of art . . .'. It was, no doubt, to give such a lead that in 1841 Chantrell designed the monument to Ralph Thoresby for Leeds Parish Church 'so as to exhibit a model of what a Gothic monument ought to be'.[53] It reuses the canopy of the piscina of the fourteenth-century church.

While antiquaries continued to debate the architectural designs in abstract terms, men like Sidgewick and Hook faced up to the practical challenge of church building. Yet so thoroughly were the views of the Ecclesiologists to be accepted from the middle of the nineteenth century that Leeds Parish Church was indeed seen as 'an historical monument' rather than an example worthy of imitation.[54] Nevertheless, before the middle of the century, it should not be forgotten that, in the absence of any dominant authority, it was a small group of architects, with whom Chantrell must be included, who first linked new ideas about ritual with medieval architectural forms to produce successful, modern buildings. The criticism of the Camdenians did little to diminish Chantrell's standing amongst churchmen in the north of England in the 1840s.

Chantrell's popularity with his patrons remained high for a further reason, and one which highlights the gulf between theory and practice referred to above. To build in the manner favoured by the Ecclesiologists was expensive, but rarely was a large budget available for church building, and Chantrell seems always to have done his utmost to tailor his proposals to the means of the client. For instance there are numerous stylistic similarities between Chantrell's All Saints at Rise (E. Riding) (Plate 19(a)) and All Saints, Roberttown, near Huddersfield (Plate 19(b)), yet the former, paid for by a wealthy landowner, cost more than twice as much as the church erected in the industrial community of Roberttown – and the latter contained more than double the number of seats at Rise. Wherever possible Chantrell would reuse old materials and build on existing foundations as an economy measure. For rebuilding Holy Trinity, Leven, he suggested, 'the body of the church can be taken down and the materials used in the new building',[55] and by this means a 'new'

---

[53] *LI*, 23 Oct. 1841.
[54] *Ibid.*
[55] University of York, Borthwick Institute, Faculty Papers, 1843/2.

church to seat 274 people could, he estimated, be produced for the incredibly low sum of less than £1,000. In the rebuilding of the parish churches of Leeds and Leven Chantrell saved as much of the old fabric as was possible. Yet his willingness to reuse materials was not, however, wholly concerned with economy, for it clearly related to his antiquarian interests. At Leeds Parish Church it was Chantrell who insisted that the workmen engaged in the demolition of the old church should save any stones which had carved patterns on them. Indeed, he rewarded the men from his own pocket for the most interesting of them from which he was able to reassemble an Anglo-Saxon cross. At Leven, his reuse of the stone did not simply provide the masons with an easily accessible quarry, but wherever possible the old carved stones were positioned exactly as they had been before, in relationship to each other, so that the new church followed, to a considerable extent, the form and size of the old one.

We have seen already that Chantrell, from the 1820s, had been looking seriously at medieval structures and using some elements of what he saw in his own work. Thus he was exceptionally well placed to capitalise on the growing interest in Gothic architecture in the 1840s, and was seen as an authority on it. Yet what is most significant in any assessment of him is that he had been engaged in similar activities for the previous ten years. The key feature of this aspect of his work is that during the period when Leeds Parish Church was being rebuilt Chantrell merely continued to exercise his established interest in archaeology; it was the response of the public, especially those concerned with the building and maintenance of churches, that was changing. Initially Chantrell's interest in archaeology was idiosyncratic; a change of attitude was needed for his knowledge to be valued widely. Thus, while few cared about his work on old churches in the 1830s, similar activities in the 1840s created public interest. For instance, while he was working at Guiseley in 1832–34 the church was described as 'dilapidated' and was seen as a burden on the ratepayers. Chantrell proposed rebuilding the north wall in a manner much more sympathetic to the rest of this interesting medieval church and his proposals would have produced a significant increase in accommodation without the expenditure of a large sum of money. Nevertheless, the parishioners settled on the cheaper alternative of filling the chancel with pews, even though they had their backs to the altar, and left the north wall untouched until it collapsed in the 1850s. Conversely, Chantrell's work at Adel in the 1840s which involved rebuilding the chancel roof on the evidence of the surviving fragments of Norman roof trusses, was the subject of much interest.[56]

His work as a restorer provided Chantrell with a major source of medieval details for inclusion in his designs for new churches. At the same time, the practical skills he developed in building new churches enriched the resources on which he could draw when faced with problems in restoration. Furthermore, the articles which he wrote dealing with the discoveries he had made in his restorations were, on one level, a part of a growing body of literature which helped to generate a general interest in old buildings, and, on another level, helped to strengthen his position as an authority in this field which in turn led to further commissions. This is shown clearly when, for example, his various works in the Norman style are considered together. It would seem that his first working acquaintance with the style came at Adel in 1838, when he was asked to repair the roof and west gable (Plate 20(a)). His work here, no doubt, brought home to him the possibilities which the style offered in terms of both economy and character. When asked to design a small church at Shadwell in 1840, he suggested using the Norman style and erected a church which cost a mere £871 (Plate 20(b)). Between these two commissions he had produced his remarkable design for the 100-feet-high termination to the twelfth century tower of Bruges Cathedral partially destroyed by fire in July 1839 (Plate 21 (b)). While Shadwell is a cautious essay in this 'new' style, adhering fairly closely to the precedent of Adel, Bruges shows him exploring the dramatic possibilities of the idiom. The Bruges design had definite sources: 'It is of very massive proportions and 250 feet high[57] with the detailed decoration resembling the towers of Ely, Norwich, Rochester and Durham (of Norman character) . . .',[58] yet Chantrell had moulded these into an original composition.

In 1843 he was again working at Adel; on this occasion reconstructing the chancel roof. The publication of his findings helped to make known his work in this field and subsequently helped him to secure appointments to advise on the state of the Norman church at East Ardsley (near Leeds) (1843) and restore the

---

[56] Revd W. H. Lewthwaite, the rector, who invited Chantrell to investigate the roof, read a paper to the Yorkshire Architectural Society on 23 April 1843, only days after the discovery. Chantrell read a paper on the old roof to the Institute of British Architects in 1847: Leeds Central Reference Library, Yorkshire Architectural Society Papers, 1843–1888, p. 110.

[57] This figure includes 150 feet of the original tower.

[58] *LI*, 30 Oct. 1847.

churches from the same period at Fangfoss (E. Riding) (c. 1849–50) and Malton (N. Riding) (1858). It would, however, be a mistake to imagine that Chantrell became an antiquary, more concerned with scholarly than practical matters of building. During this period he was engaged on a significant number of commissions to repair relatively recent churches designed by Taylor, Atkinson and others. In these it was his task to sort out such mundane, yet serious, problems as dry-rot, and leaking roofs. At the same time limited budgets dictated that his new churches had to be extremely cheap. His estimate of 1838 for rebuilding Pool church was a mere £308; it is no wonder that the Gothic embellishments were applied sparingly and that there was no opportunity to build a chancel; the altar being placed against the 'east' wall. Building work was carried out in 1839–40, the finished building consisting of a body with a low tower and spire at the west end.

If the analysis of Chantrell's churches of this period is broadened to include those at, say, Honley (Plates 21(a) and 22(a)), Leven or Cowling, it is clear that in all of them he worked to produce a building as large, as dignified and as archaeologically correct as the budget would allow and each is successful within these limitations. However, the churches discussed in this section, whose designs are more or less concurrent with the rebuilding of Leeds Parish Church, form an oddly assorted group and it is difficult to trace any sort of coherence when their designs are considered together. It seems that each one represented an individual response to the circumstances of its commission. By 1842 Chantrell had acquired all the knowledge of church-planning and detailing that he was ever likely to need; what he still lacked was identification of the basic principle which lay behind the designs of the ancient buildings he so much admired.

1842–1847

The year 1842 is a significant one in Chantrell's personal development as a church architect; in that year he formulated a theory which he believed explained the system of proportions used by medieval architects. This had a marked effect on his own church designs, but, before these are discussed, it is worth pausing to examine the theory and its significance within the small, but then expanding, body of literature on the subject. It is an area of archaeological scholarship in which Chantrell occupies a position of national importance. Prior to his 'discovery', Chantrell admitted that he had 'worked without system – merely adapting ancient features to masses, to which [he] could give no just proportion'.[59] Chantrell certainly found this an unsatisfactory way of designing, a point that had been anticipated by Thomas Kerrick in 1809, in a paper read to the Archaeological Institute of Great Britain and Ireland: '[Until] the principles and rules by which [medieval churches] were designed . . . are discovered, all our attempts to build in the Gothic style must be unsuccessful . . .'.[60] For generations of architects and theorists trained to accept the importance of rules in Classical architecture, there seemed little doubt that the medieval architects had been guided by equally cogent principles, 'but unhappily no medieval Vitruvius had collected and transmitted them'.[61] At least, no written record of them was known in the early nineteenth century.[62] John Mason Neale and Benjamin Webb, two key early members of the Camden Society, were voicing widely-held views in believing ancient builders possessed 'some Canons of church Symbolism, now unknown to us', but which had been 'a rule and precedent to architects of the past'.[63] Neale went on to state: 'That there is a proportion observed between every part of an ancient church is an unquestionable fact; we feel and know it to be so, though we cannot at present explain its rules, nor analyse its principles'.[64] Pugin was one of the few writers in this period who did feel capable of offering an explanation and stated unhesitatingly that he had 'discovered [the medieval architect's] laws of pointed design'. However, the enquiring reader would have been disappointed to find that Pugin could offer nothing more informative than that 'beauty of architectural design depended on its being the expression of what the building required, and that for Christians that expression could only be correctly given by the medium of pointed architecture . . .'.[65] A writer in the *Ecclesiologist* was perhaps correct in concluding

[59] *Builder*, V (1847), p.300.
[60] Published in *Archaeologia*, XVI (1812), p.298.
[61] C. R. Cockerell, 'William of Wykeham', *Proceedings at the Annual Meeting of the Archaeological Institute . . . at Winchester, 1845* (1846), p.32.
[62] *Archaeologia*, XVI (1812), p.298. He suggests that if the theory had been written down, the books 'probably perished in the reformation'.
[63] J. M. Neale and B. Webb, *The Symbolism of Churches and Church Ornament: A Translation of . . . Durandus . . .* (Cambridge, 1843), pp.lxxiv–lxxxv, quoted in J. F. White, *The Cambridge Movement* (Oxford, 1979), pp.81–82.
[64] J. M. Neale, *Church Enlargement and Church Arrangement* (Cambridge, 1843), p.8, quoted in White, p.82.
[65] A. W. N. Pugin, *The True Principles of Pointed or Christian Architecture . . .* (1841), p.9.

that Pugin's own idea of perfection was an absolute copy of a medieval building',[66] which would have conveniently relieved Pugin of the necessity of considering the principles of proportion on which Gothic architecture had been based. However, there was a number of people who did wish to understand the proportional system which it was assumed medieval architects had used. Since the buildings which were presumed to have been based on this mysterious system existed in large numbers, it is not surprising that there were attempts from about 1800[67] to rediscover the principles by working back from the measurements of these buildings. It was a task undertaken by what P. H. Scholfield refers to as 'a small group of enthusiasts'[68] of whom Chantrell was an important member. Scholfield sees the wider significance of this group as stemming from their having inaugurated 'the shift of interest from arithmetic and the analytical study of linear proportions to geometry and the study of shape'.[69] Dominating the various early nineteenth-century theories of medieval proportion is a shape known as the *vesica piscis*.[70] The importance that was attached to it then no doubt stemmed from Cesariano's commentary to his translation of Vitruvius of 1521. This was hardly a primary medieval source yet, in the absence of anything of significance that was older, it represented a useful starting point for a study of medieval proportional systems. Cesariano mentioned three rules that had been used in the designing of Gothic churches. The first fixed the overall length and breadth of the church by means of the *vesica piscis*; the second provided for the subdivision of the plan into equal bays; and the third determined the heights of the various parts by means of equilateral triangles.[71] The figure had been discussed by Dürer in 1525,[72] and its earliest consideration in the nineteenth century was probably Kerrick's paper, read to the Archaeological Institute in 1820.[73] Between this date and 1842 when Chantrell discovered his

---

[66] *Ecclesiologist*, XIII (1852), 552.

[67] C. R. Cockerell, 'William of Wykeham'. 'We have sought them for half a century', he wrote in 1845.

[68] P. H. Scholfield, *The Theory of Proportion in Architecture* (Cambridge, 1958), p.82.

[69] *Ibid.*, p.84.

[70] The construction of the figure is fully explained in J. Gwilt, *An Encyclopaedia of Architecture* (1888), pp.1010–11. The main early nineteenth-century writings on the subject were listed in Gwilt, p.1008 *et seq.*, and Scholfield, p.82 *et seq.*

[71] Scholfield, pp.86–87.

[72] Gwilt, p.1009.

[73] Published in *Archaeologia*, XIX (1821), pp.353–68.

system,[74] little attention seems to have been devoted to the problem. John Browne of York had been working on the subject and had shown Chantrell his findings 'about 1830',[75] and R. W. Billings published his *Attempt to Define the Geometric Proportions . . .* in 1840,[76] but these are possibly the extent of the early investigations of the subject in England and show the pioneering nature of Chantrell's contribution.

Plate 18(b) shows Chantrell's system and as Joseph Gwilt notes, 'if it be drawn out to a very much larger scale it will not appear so complex'. Gwilt goes on to describe the construction of the system as follows:

> Besides the triangles, the points are obtained for many polygons. The six divisions AA, BB, from the semi-diameter are first obtained; and straight lines drawn to each alternate one give triangles. On their intersections, as CC, if lines be continued to the circumference, six centres are given, DD, FF, upon which, with the first radius AB (or of the semi-diameter), strike a second series of segments, and a third set of 12 centres is obtained. The second centres will give two intersecting triangles, completing the first part of the design. Upon the 24 points of the intersecting inner arcs, a circle inscribed will determine the inner triangles upon the centres of the first, and the diagram is perfected. For more complex forms, an additional number of centre lines may be drawn upon the remaining intersections.[77]

Chantrell, like other architects of his generation trained in the Classical style, was thoroughly educated in the importance of rules and proportion in the Classical orders. Yet Soane's own views on proportion echo the 'Romantic' tendencies prevalent in early nineteenth-century art. '[Architecture] has no fixed proportion. Taste, good sense and sound judgement must direct the mind of the architect to apply harmony and justice of relative proportion, the

---

[74] Gwilt gives this date (p. 1015) and in 'The Description of the church of Saint Philip, Leeds', which appeared in the *LI*, 9 Oct. 1847, and was almost certainly written by Chantrell, it is stated, 'The proportions are obtained on a system discovered in 1842 by . . . Mr Chantrell'. Whether the system was modified before being discussed in the paper Chantrell delivered to the Institute of British Architects in 1847, and which appeared in the *Builder* in the same year, is not clear.

[75] *Builder*, V (1847), p. 301. Browne's system does not appear to have been published.

[76] Noted in J. Gwilt, p. 1011.

[77] *Ibid.*, p. 1015.

correlation of the parts with the whole, and of the whole with each part.'[78]

Batty Langley's *Gothic Architecture, improved by Rules and Proportions, . . .* of 1742 had been thoroughly discredited long before Chantrell started to practice and, like other church architects of the early nineteenth century, Chantrell initially followed Soane's advice, and relied on an essentially subjective approach to proportion. The individual nature of the buildings he produced before 1842 suggest that he was, in fact, working unsystematically; a state of affairs he surely found unsatisfactory.

There are two additional factors which might have encouraged Chantrell to study the subject of proportion in medieval architecture: first, his involvement with Freemasonry, and second, his contact with the Huddersfield architect, William Wallen. The mystical nature of proportion and measurement forms an essential part of the ritual of Freemasonry, and from the late 1830s Chantrell was involved with the craft. On 7 June 1837 he had joined the Lodge of Unanimity, No. 179, in Wakefield[79] and on 21 June 1838 he became a member of the Lodge of Fidelity, in Leeds.[80] The ritual does not describe the system which guided medieval 'masons' but states that they, like the architects in other great civilisations, had used 'a' system. It is possible that this was sufficient to encourage Chantrell to pursue the subject; in writing about his church at Rise (1844–45), Chantrell stated the design 'was founded on true masonic principles'.[81] He was no doubt aware of some of the earlier writers who had tried to prove that it was the Freemasons who had been the guardians of the secrets of proportion. These authors believed that small groups of Freemasons had travelled throughout Europe applying the principles to the great cathedrals they built and in this way ensured a uniformity of proportion in all of them.[82]

In April 1842 William Wallen wrote to the Commissioners for Building New Churches: 'Sir, I shall feel gratified by your acceptance of the accompanying pamphlet being an attempt to prove from

---

[78] J. Soane, *Lectures in Architecture*, ed. A. T. Bolton (1929), p. 100.

[79] John Goodchild Collection, Wakefield: List of Joining Members of the Lodge of Unanimity. His membership was witnessed by Charles Clapham, a surveyor and architect in Wakefield.

[80] A. Scarth, and C. A. Brown, *History of the Lodge of Fidelity* (1894), p. 220.

[81] *Civil Engineer and Architect's Journal*, April 1846, p. 100.

[82] The issue is discussed in detail in *Gould's History of Freemasonry*, ed. D. Wright (1931), pp. 120–41. It concludes that there is no evidence for believing that these Freemasons had any exclusive access to ecclesiastical commissions nor that they all subscribed to any precise theory of proportion.

existing remains and actual measurements, the existence of Geometric Principles in the structures of the middle ages'.[83] Sadly, the 'accompanying pamphlet' is no longer with the letter and its precise content is unknown. However, it seems unlikely that it could be only a coincidence that two architects from the West Riding would be working on the same subject simultaneously. Is it possible that they worked together and, since Wallen's theory appeared in print five years before Chantrell's, was it Wallen who introduced Chantrell to the subject and perhaps supplied him with some of his initial ideas? There is an almost total absence of material about Chantrell's dealings with his fellow architects yet there is some indication that a relationship existed between him and Wallen.[84]

But this is all speculation. What is clear is that Chantrell was dissatisfied with 'working without system', and by 1842 had developed a theory which he believed explained the way in which medieval architects worked, and which could be used for the design of new buildings in the Gothic style. On 7 April 1843 he read a paper to the Leeds Philosophical and Literary Society 'On the Geometric Principles of Gothic Architecture,'[85] and on 14 June 1847 delivered a paper 'On the Geometric System applied by the Medieval Architects to the Proportions of Ecclesiastical Structures' to the Institute of British Architects.[86] An article with the same title subsequently appeared in the *Builder*.[87]

Thomas Kerrick's essay seems to have been the starting point for Chantrell's enquiries[88] but he soon found that this system had only limited application. It satisfactorily explained the form of a number of medieval churches, but Chantrell found that there were plans to which it could not be applied, and he concluded that 'Mr Kerrick's theory cannot be admitted further than as a small integral part of a more general and comprehensive system'.[89] Similarly, Browne's theory, which concerned the use of the circle, could be 'proved' by its application to certain plans, but the existence of arrangements which it did not fit led Chantrell to conclude that this could not be considered 'a universal system'.[90] Clearly, for a system to be

[83] CBC, file no.21744, part 9.
[84] Webster, p.374.
[85] *LI*, 15 April 1843.
[86] *Gentleman's Magazine* 28, pt ii (1847), pp.68–69.
[87] *Builder*, V (1847), pp.300–02.
[88] However, Chantrell appears to have read it only after the completion of Leeds Parish Church: *ibid*., p.300.
[89] *Ibid*., p.301.
[90] *Ibid*.

applicable to all examples, it needed a wider range of points formed by the intersection of constructed lines or arcs, and into which a medieval plan could be shown to fit. This is precisely what Chantrell's system offered. It was capable of producing an almost infinite number of equilateral triangles within concentric circles of different radii, and Chantrell maintained that, 'this system will apply to the works of all ages that can be tested by sound geometric principles'.[91]

In the light of subsequent studies on the subject, how valid was Chantrell's theory? In discussing Kerrick's system, Scholfield wrote: 'Having provided himself by an entirely arbitrary process with a wide enough range of rectangles, he needs only what Nobbs calls a "little selective adroitness" to apply them to small-scale drawings with which his paper is profusely illustrated.'[92] If the criticism is valid for Kerrick's system, it is even more so for Chantrell's which provided a greatly increased range of shapes into which its author could 'prove' medieval plans would fit. Indeed he allowed himself additional flexibility by noting that one of the key lines generated by his system 'may either pass through the centre of the [line of] piers or come on the outer or inner faces [of them] . . .'.[93] Scholfield stated that the available evidence suggests that

> medieval architects were keenly interested in geometry and in its application to the problem of proportion in the widest sense of the word. But it is doubtful whether this interest got beyond the formulation of arbitrary rules for the setting-out of the general lines of buildings on the one hand, and the explanation of the symmetry of geometrical form and pattern on the other hand.[94]

This broadly agrees with B. G. Morgan's view that '. . . medieval design may have been founded on geometrical concepts. However, there is nothing to suggest that some single geometrical figure contains the secret of all Gothic architecture'.[95] 'The critical weakness in the nineteenth-century theories . . . is not that they held geometry

[91] *Ibid.*, p.302.
[92] P. Scholfield, p.88.
[93] J. Gwilt, p.1015. This is explained in Plate 18(b) which Chantrell interpreted as follows: 'M is part of the plan of the nave of Boston Church, Lincolnshire, arranged on the former principle, while N is part of that of Middleton-on-the-Wolds Church, Yorkshire, where the lines come on the inner face of the piers'.
[94] Scholfield, p.87.
[95] B. G. Morgan, *Canonic Design in English Medieval Architecture* (Liverpool, 1961), p.17.

to be at the heart of medieval architecture, but that, in spite of a lack of support from contemporaneous documentary sources, they regarded the great monuments as unified compositions derived from a predetermined arrangement of geometrical figures.'[96] One can point to George Lesser[97] as an example of a modern writer who is committed to a belief in the importance of geometry in religious architecture but more important here than the state of the current debate about the subjects is the mid nineteenth-century attitude to it. In the later editions of Gwilt's highly successful *An Encyclopaedia of Architecture*, which first appeared in 1842, Chantrell's theory is fully discussed in the section on 'Modern Investigations [into Proportional Systems]'. It follows accounts of theories of Kerrick, R. W. Billings and C. R. Cockerell and receives as much coverage as any of the others, and continued to do so until at least the edition of 1888.

Cockerell's interest in the subject can only have added to the prestige of Chantrell's work. In 1845, during Cockerell's tenure of the professorship of architecture at the Royal Academy, he read a paper to the Archaeological Institute of Great Britain and Ireland on 'William of Wykeham'.[98] In this he suggested medieval architects had used the *vesica piscis* extensively, and demonstrated this with reference to William of Wykeham's buildings. If Chantrell did fully develop his theory by 1842 it is not certain that Cockerell knew of it; nevertheless the latter's work on the subject denotes the exclusive nature of the group in which Chantrell found himself through his archaeological studies.

To what extent did Chantrell's discovery affect the churches he designed after 1842? We know from his writings that the principles were certainly put into practice. 'I have now some new churches in progress on this principle – "first pointed" at Halifax [King Cross]; "second" (decorated), at Huddersfield [Armitage Bridge]; and at Leeds; "third" or perpendicular, at Keighley . . .',[99] he wrote in March 1846, and the following year he stated that upon 'this system, with great advantage and satisfaction, I have had erected the churches of Leven and Rise, in Holderness, Middleton near Leeds [Plate 22(b)], King Cross, in Halifax [Plate 23(a)]; and those of St Paul, Armitage Bridge, near Huddersfield, and St Philip's, in Leeds [Plate

[96] *Ibid.*, p. 16.
[97] G. Lesser, *Gothic Cathedrals and Sacred Geometry* (1957).
[98] Later published in *Proceedings at the Annual Meeting of the Archaeological Institute of Great Britain and Ireland at Winchester, MDCCCXLX*, 1846. See also Watkin, pp. 125–28.
[99] *Civil Engineer and Architect's Journal*, April 1846, p. 100.

23(b)], are rapidly advancing towards completion'.[100] It is therefore not unreasonable to add a further two churches on which he was working in this period, and which are thus likely to have been designed on the same 'principles'. They are St Paul, Denholme Gate, near Halifax, and All Saints, Roberttown, near Huddersfield (Plate 19(b)).[101] These nine churches[102] were designed between 1842 and 1845 and are his last 'new' churches. Unlike the pre-1842 churches, they form a stylistically unified group, but it would be a mistake to expect them to appear similar. Indeed it was the capacity for variety within the principle which Chantrell saw as a major advantage of this method of designing. '[Rise Church] is founded upon true masonic principles, even to the mouldings, nothing strictly copied, but composed. No two buildings are to be found alike, – and why? Simply for this reason: That the principle, on having the key, is inexhaustible; and, by working upon the key, minutes will suffice to produce new subjects, where days may be expended in copying . . .'.[103] Certainly Chantrell believed he had found his longed-for 'system' to work within and thus was able to go beyond 'merely adapting ancient features to masses . . .'.[104] Whatever shortcomings his 'system' may be shown to have, it cannot be denied that his writings are a confident statement of his mastery of the problem of composition. More importantly, his buildings of this period are an accomplished and assured series of Gothic essays, which suggest the system was capable of practical application, at least for Chantrell.

The value of the 'system' was enhanced by the range of church designs to which Chantrell successfully applied it. It included the styles Early English, Decorated and Perpendicular, as well as sizes which range from small (Rise) (Plate 19(a)), to large (Keighley) (Plates 24(a) and (b)), and costs which varied from cheap (Roberttown) (Plate 19(b)), to expensive (Armitage Bridge). Further-more, it seems it was even possible to adapt it to the constraints of

[100] *Builder*, V (1847), p. 302.
[101] The church was designed by Chantrell and, initially, its erection was supervised by J. B. Chantrell and Shaw. When this partnership was dissolved, in February 1845, Shaw assumed responsibility for its completion.
[102] These are, in an approximate chronological order of design: Holy Trinity, Leven, designed (?) 1842; St Paul, Denholme Gate, designed early 1843; All Saints, Roberttown, designed mid 1843; St Paul, King Cross, designed (?) early 1844; All Saints, Rise, designed before April 1844; Saint Paul, Armitage Bridge, designed late 1844; Saint Andrew, Keighley, designed early 1845; St Philip, Leeds, designed early 1845; St Mary, Middleton, designed early 1845.
[103] *Civil Engineer and Architect's Journal*, April 1846, p. 100.
[104] *Builder*, V (1847), p. 300.

small and irregular sites, for example at St Philip, Leeds (Plate 23(b)). The two Leeds churches, St Philip's and St Mary's (Middleton) (Plate 22(b)), are typical of those in the group. St Mary's, which consists of a chancel, nave (originally intended to have a clerestory), aisles and a tower projecting from the south aisle and forming the south porch, apparently demonstrates how the principle could be adapted, with successful results, to a medium-sized church of unorthodox plan. But is the high quality of all these designs due solely to their proportions? It is instructive to look back to a typical example of Chantrell's earlier Early English churches, St Peter's, Morley, (Plate 14(a)) and compare it with St Mary's, Middleton. Many of the details have changed little in the near twenty years which separate the two designs, for example the spires and the top stages of the towers are similar and the west wall of Middleton has a number of things in common with the east wall of Morley. Nevertheless, in essence the churches are different. Certainly the proportions of Middleton are more satisfactory; but it is not a deeper understanding of proportions alone which prompted Chantrell to include buttresses at Middleton in places where they are absent at Morley, or to site the tower of Middleton on the south rather than the west side, as at Morley. Is not the greater visual success of Middleton to a considerable extent the result of the essentially subjective judgements which Chantrell formed after the careful study of countless medieval churches, rather than the objective application of a system of proportion?

In the 1840s, the more progressive commentators on medieval architecture were admiring it, in part, for its picturesque qualities, qualities which are usually felt to be absent from Gothic work of the earlier nineteenth century. The essential difference between Morley and Middleton is that the former is a classical composition of more or less Gothic details while the latter exhibits a greater understanding of Gothic details, arranged according to Chantrell's system of proportions; but ultimately the design is controlled by a sophisticated appreciation of picturesque principles of composition.

It was no doubt the experience of designing St Philip's – where the extremely cramped site ruled out a conventional western tower – which brought home to Chantrell the picturesque possibilities of an asymmetrically-placed tower, and suggested to him the advantages of placing St Mary's tower adjacent to the south aisle. Both churches were designed in the spring of 1845 and the plans are in many ways similar. The foundation stone of St Mary's was laid on 28 July 1845[105] and it was consecrated on 22 September 1846.[106] At St Philip's the foundation stone was laid on 10 November 1845[107] and it was dedicated in the autumn of 1847.[108] Chantrell described the style of St Philip's as 'after the earlier part of the 14th century when pointed architecture was rising towards perfection'. As if to stress the importance of his 'geometrical principles' he adds that this is a style 'which modern architects can not expect to attain without studying the principles with the same devotion as did their medieval predecessors . . .'.[109]

---

[105] *LI*, 26 July 1845.
[106] *LI*, 26 Sept. 1846.
[107] *LI*, 1 Nov. 1845.
[108] The *LI* of 9 Oct. 1847 says that the church has 'just been dedicated'.
[109] *LI*, 9 Oct. 1847.

CHAPTER 5

The Rebuilding of Leeds Parish Church

St Peter's, the parish church of Leeds, is the most important of
Chantrell's buildings. Its importance for him lay not simply in its
size or cost, but in his successful handling of the project which
transformed his otherwise flagging career. However, it was a success
in which all the churchmen of Leeds shared, for during the course
of rebuilding it came to be seen as a symbol of the revival of church
life in the town, and its congregations were justifiably proud of
their spiritual and architectural achievements. At the time of its
consecration the *Church Intelligencer* summarised these factors:

> We trust we shall have no more churches built in the
> bald and beggarly style of dissenting meeting-houses,
> unworthy of God and discreditable to those who build
> them, but of the manner of the magnificent church at
> Leeds which stands a noble monument to the taste, the
> sterling Christianity, and the old-fashioned piety and
> spirit of Churchmanship of that town.[1]

The commission is exceptionally well documented and, while it
cannot be considered as typical of Chantrell's ecclesiastical work by
virtue of its size, it forms a useful case study and illuminates a
number of aspects of his professional practice.

The old church (Plate 25(a)) which Chantrell demolished was
described by Thoresby as

> a very spacious and strong fabrick . . . it doth not pretend
> to the Mode of the Reformed Architecture but is strong
> and useful . . . plain but venerable . . . it is built in the
> Manner of a Cathedral, with a large cross Aisle and a
> Steeple or Tower in the middle of it. The dimensions of
> the church are, length 165 foot, Breadth 97, Height of
> the Nave of the Church 51, and of the Steeple 96.[2]

---

[1] *Church Intelligencer*, 11 Sept. 1841.
[2] R. Thoresby, *Ducatus Leodiensis*, 2nd edn. (Leeds, 1816), p.39ff.

Although fragments of an earlier building were included, the 'nave and tower seem to have dated from the mid fourteenth century, the chancel from the late fifteenth; and a fourth nave aisle had been added in the early sixteenth century'.[3] Alterations continued to be made in the seventeenth and eighteenth centuries but these were far from sympathetic to the medieval structure and included 'for the double purpose of increasing still more the accommodation, and giving the organ a conspicuous position, the chancel arch was nearly walled up and a gallery erected against it, in which the organ was set up in 1714'.[4] (Plate 25(b)). Thus the church was virtually divided into two quite distinct parts: the western half crowded with pews and containing the pulpit; and the eastern section left as a vast but barren expense devoid of seats, with the altar 'enclosed by a bold oak screen of Italian design',[5] below the bricked-up east window.[6] This separation was, not surprisingly, found by many to be objectionable. The chancel was virtually unusable, except at the time of Holy Communion, since anyone placed there could not see the pulpit. Furthermore, the congregation seated in the nave could not see the altar, making it difficult for the officiating minister to follow the rubric of the Communion service.[7] Indeed several of the nave pews even had their backs to the altar. To obtain the maximum accommodation in the nave, not only was the floor cluttered with irregularly shaped pews, but galleries had been erected on all four sides. Their construction had necessitated cutting into the fourteenth-century columns and arches as well as the creation of large and incongruous dormer windows to light the gallery stairs.[8]

By the early nineteenth century, not only was the internal arrangement unsatisfactory, but also the structure of the building required repair. The *Leeds Intelligencer* of 31 July 1809 stated, 'It having been judged necessary to re-edify some parts of St Peter's in this town, the church wardens have, much to their credit, been actively engaged in the necessary works for some time past'. This included the rebuilding of part of the south wall, the work being superintended by the Leeds architect Thomas Taylor. His principal window in the south transept was described as 'exhibiting a beautiful

[3] Linstrum, p.169.
[4] R. W. Moore, *A History of the Parish Church of Leeds*, (Leeds, 1877). p.4.
[5] *Ibid.*
[6] E. K. Clark, *Leeds Parish Church* (1931), p.6.
[7] Moore, p.4.
[8] *Ibid.*

spectrum of Gothic architecture'[9] and it was filled with stained glass by Jacob Wright, also of Leeds. The project was completed in 1812.

While this work was in progress, serious concern was expressed as to the soundness of the tower. 'It is judged proper to state that upon examination of the pillars and aisles upon which the steeple is erected, there does not appear any grounds for [the belief that the foundations are unsatisfactory]. However, the heavy set of bells will not be rung for the present'.[10] Furthermore, the vicar was urged to appoint 'some respectable architect'[11] to examine and survey the tower and make a report on its state. It is interesting that Taylor, currently engaged in rebuilding the south wall, was not the 'respectable architect' engaged. The task was given to Charles Weston of York, the leading Yorkshire architect in the first decade of the nineteenth century, who was 'recommended by the archdeacon',[12] and who presented his report in June 1810. He stated he had found a 'large crack' in the tower and that the tower's construction was of rubble walling on the inside, unlike the larger, regular stones on the outside. However, he felt it was quite safe for bell-ringing to be commenced. He advised strengthening the north-east and south-east angles and suggested that the inside of the winding staircase to the tower be repaired to prevent the stagnant air further decaying the walls. 'If this is done judiciously, there would be not a doubt in my mind of the tower standing for ages to come.'[13] Watson adds that, although not included in his letter of instructions, he felt obliged to warn the churchwardens not to allow any further cutting away of the pillars or arches for the convenience or enlargement of individual pews. 'I never saw a church so mutilated in this respect.'[14]

In the twenty-five years between the finishing of the south wall and the beginning of Chantrell's rebuilding, no work of importance was carried out on the building.

The driving force behind the reconstruction of the church was undoubtedly the new vicar, Dr Walter Farquhar Hook, who, on 20 March 1837 had been appointed to the living. On his arrival in Leeds he found the town a stronghold of dissent, and the church physically and spiritually at a low ebb. By 1837 there were over 150,000 inhabitants in the town, yet only fifty communicants at the

[9] *LI*, 11 May 1812.
[10] *LI*, 7 May 1810.
[11] *Ibid.*
[12] *LI*, 25 June 1810.
[13] *Ibid.*
[14] *Ibid.*

parish church.[15] As a 'high' churchman, he must have been dismayed at the near total abandonment of the chancel and the neglect of the decorative parts of the building which had survived from the medieval period. However, the general decay of the structure and the ugly appearance of the building was such as to dismay any incumbent, no matter how little he cared about ritual and architecture. Two years before Hook came to the town, *A Walk through Leeds*, a guidebook aimed at the general reader, was no doubt expressing widely held views when it described part of the church thus: 'The West front has a lofty pointed window of four lights, comparatively modern (the fine old stone tracery being removed in 1708) and very clumsy; the other windows at this end have almost as remote a pretension to beauty . . . the clerestory has three mean windows . . .'.[16] In Chantrell's opinion 'the only portion [of the old church] possessing character was one window at the north-east corner, of the time of Henry the Seventh, with a depressed arch, and cusped tracery; some water spouts carved into grotesque figures, and some fragments of pinnacles on the north front . . .'.[17] A lesser man than Hook might have been daunted by the task of trying to restore the position of the established church in the town and repair the ageing structure from which he was to work. However, he was a man of tireless energy and commitment; 'the greatest parish priest of the 19th century'[18] who saw these two tasks as inter-related. He believed 'a handsome church [was] a kind of standing sermon',[19] and thus within two weeks of his induction on 15 April 1837, he had already begun to consider the restoration of the parish church as the first move towards a revival of Anglicanism in the town. The *Intelligencer* reported on 29 April 1837:

> A speedy improvement of the interior of the Parish Church . . . is likely to take place. The body of the edifice should be repewed, by which nearly one half more sittings might be obtained; and the north gallery must be set back, but before this can be done, the roof over the north aisle will require raising about 12 feet. We have heard that the entire expense would not exceed £2,000 to £2,500.

[15] J. Rusby, *History of the Parish Church of St Peter at Leeds* (Leeds, 1896), p.66.
[16] J. Heaton, *Walk through Leeds*, p.32.
[17] R. D. Chantrell, 'Discoveries made in taking down the Parish Church of Leeds', in *Votive Offerings*, ed. T. Furbank (1839), p.162.
[18] J. Rusby, *A History of the Parish Church of Leeds* (Leeds, 1877), p.6.
[19] *LI*, 11 Nov. 1837.

By the beginning of October that year, much grander things were envisaged.

> A plan is in contemplation by which the Parish Church may be so improved as to accommodate 1,200 more persons than at present . . . the plan embraces the removal and rebuilding of the tower, the removal of the organ, raising the roof so as to admit of setting back of the north gallery, the transference of the pulpit to a better place, and refitting up the whole of the inside of the edifice. The cost is estimated at £4,500.[20]

So far, it seems these ideas were the vicar's. He had a meeting with some of the leading gentlemen of the town at John Gott's house on 19 October 1837,[21] and it was the host who suggested he procure plans from Chantrell.[22] The latter appears immediately to have influenced the proposed scheme as only two days after this meeting the *Intelligencer* reported the intention of 'raising the whole roof . . . [and making] a new arrangement of entire internal economy of the edifice . . .'.[23] Furthermore, the anticipated cost had by this time risen to £6,000.[24] The following week, the vicar and trustees met and resolved that it was 'highly desirable to carry into effect as soon as possible, the enlargement'. A plan of the proposed alterations drawn up by Mr Chantrell, the architect, under the direction of the vicar was exhibited and the cost was estimated at £6,000.[25] An enthusiastic meeting on 8 November 1837 heard the vicar say

> that certain repairs are necessary – that certain great alterations are necessary to the Parish Church – as no-one who looks at that church can for one half a moment can deny (Hear, hear, responded the audience). The Parish Church was described by Thoresby as "black but comely". Black, I am sorry to say, it still is, but comely it has ceased to be owing to the various alterations that have taken place from time to time – not upon any fixed plan – the convenience of individuals has been studied rather than accommodation of the public. As the church

[20] *LI*, 7 Oct. 1837.
[21] Moore, p.6.
[22] *LI*, 23 Oct. 1841.
[23] *LI*, 21 Oct. 1837.
[24] *Ibid.*
[25] *LI*, 28 Oct. 1837.

PLATE 25 (a)   LEEDS PARISH CHURCH.
Watercolour by J. Rhodes showing the old church which Chantrell demolished.

PLATE 25 (b)   LEEDS PARISH CHURCH.
Watercolour showing the nave of the old church.

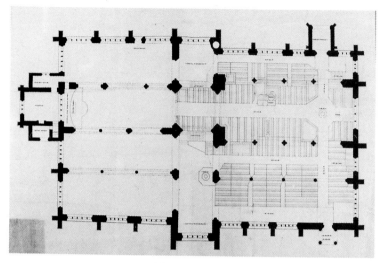

PLATE 26 (a)   LEEDS PARISH CHURCH.
Ground plan by Chantrell, November 1837, showing the old church.

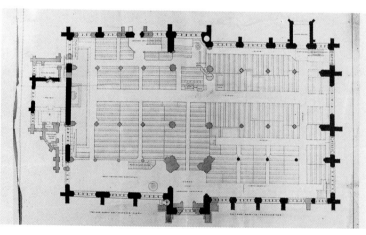

PLATE 26 (b)   LEEDS PARISH CHURCH.
Ground plan by Chantrell, November 1837, showing the proposed alterations.

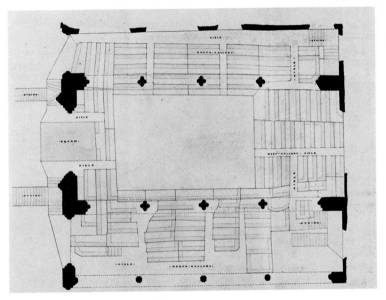

PLATE 27 (a)   LEEDS PARISH CHURCH.
Gallery plan by Chantrell, November 1837, of the old church.

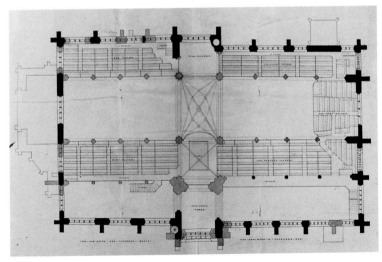

PLATE 27 (b)   LEEDS PARISH CHURCH.
Gallery plan by Chantrell, November 1837, showing the proposed alterations.

PLATE 28 (a)   LEEDS PARISH CHURCH, 1837–41.
Lithograph of the church from the south east.

PLATE 28 (b)   LEEDS PARISH CHURCH, 1837–41, FROM THE NORTH–EAST.
Lithograph by Richardson and Hawkins of 1841.

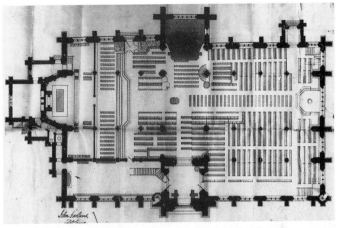

PLATE 29 (a)   LEEDS PARISH CHURCH, 1837–41.
Plan by Chantrell, 1841, showing the finished church.

PLATE 29 (b)   LEEDS PARISH CHURCH, 1837–41, INTERIOR LOOKING WEST.
Lithograph by Shaw and Groom.

PLATE 30 (a)   NETHERTHONG, WR: ALL SAINTS,
ORIGINALLY BUILT BY CHANTRELL, 1826–30.
Drawing by Chantrell for proposed rebuilding of bell turret, 1847.

PLATE 30 (b)   LOCKWOOD, NEAR HUDDERSFIELD:
EMMANUEL CHURCH,
ORIGINALLY BUILT BY CHANTRELL, 1826–30.
Chancel, also designed by Chantrell, added 1848–49.

> at present stands . . . it is quite impossible to perform
> the services of the sanctuary with order and decency . . .
> let us remember that we are to build our churches not
> only for the use of the people, but also for the glory of
> our God.[26]

It was at this meeting that Henry Hall, the churchwarden, proposed that 'Chantrell's plan be adopted'.[27] There was general agreement for this and it would appear to mark the formal appointment of Chantrell as architect for the rebuilding. Hall went on to say that he had 'paid a good deal of attention to the variety of plans which had been suggested for the enlargement of the church and after due deliberation he was of the opinion that the one now proposed was the best calculated of all for affording the greatest accommodation'. It would be interesting to know if the 'variety of plans' included others from professional architects or whether they were all from interested laymen, with the exception of Chantrell's.

Later in November the faculty was applied for and four drawings by Chantrell explained the scheme[28] (Plates 26(a)–27(b)). These showed that it was intended to 'remove the tower from the centre to the north aisle, to extend the two lines of columns in the chancel so as to give breadth equal to that of the nave and raise the roof of the north aisle retaining however the whole of the external walls, and putting new tracery into the windows . . .'.[29] The arrangement of pews in the nave and nave galleries was to be only slightly different from that which existed before 1837, but the newly widened chancel was to be filled with pews, which was the principal way in which the accommodation was to be increased. The north-east and south-east galleries were to extend to the east wall and the pews on the ground floor left only one bay free for the altar and communion rail, giving the area around the altar a distinctly cramped appearance. Although Hook has come to be seen as an enlightened church planner, at this stage the scheme followed closely the Commissioners' principle of the maximum number of seats for the least expense; it was estimated that the alterations would produce an additional 1,100 'kneelings' for the relatively modest price of

---

[26] *LI*, 11 Nov. 1837. Continuing in the same vein is the 'Sonnet on the Rebuilding of Leeds Parish Church', by H. A. Jackson, in *Votive Offerings*.

[27] *LI*, 11 Nov. 1837.

[28] Borthwick Institute, Faculty Papers 1837/5. The drawings are dated 'November 1837' but the day of the month is not recorded.

[29] *LI*, 30 Nov. 1839.

£6,300. Also interesting is that in this initial design the floor of the chancel was to be flat with only one step up to the sanctuary.

It is difficult to identify the extent of Hook's and Chantrell's contribution to this scheme, but clearly the issue is of importance. Certainly the initial ideas were Hook's, and, as has been stated already, 'the plan of the proposed alterations [was] drawn up by Mr Chantrell, under the direction of the Vicar . . .'. However, at the public meeting on 8 November 1837, when these drawings were exhibited, the vicar said '. . . on receiving this requisition [to call this meeting] I conferred with Mr Chantrell, the architect, in order to fix upon some plan . . .',[30] which does not suggest that Hook had proceeded far beyond the identification of the problems in the old church.

The 'removal' of the tower from the centre of the church can be credited to Hook and justified on two counts. First, it was in a poor condition and needed major repairs if it was to be kept in its original position, and second, if it was removed the crossing piers could be widened to produce a greater unity of space between nave and chancel, and also give those members of the congregation seated in the nave a clear view of the altar. Hook believed it essential that the congregation should be able to see and hear the officiating minister. But was the idea of placing the new tower in the centre of the north wall also Hook's? It is true that Chantrell had not previously designed a church with a tower in such a position but its placing at Leeds Parish Church displays such genius that one wonders whether it could have been the idea of anyone but Chantrell. In no other part of the church would it have had such visual impact, as, placed thus, it terminates the view along Kirkgate, the principal thoroughfare to the church, and so gives it a commanding position in the town despite being outside its centre. In this way it most effectively assumed the role of Hook's 'standing sermon'.[31]

---

[30] *LI*, 11 Nov. 1837. See also H. W. Dalton, 'Walter Farquhar Hook, Vicar of Leeds: his work for the Church and the Town, 1837–1848', *PTh.S*, LXIII (1990), 39–42.

[31] Hook had suggested the 'removal' of the tower before Chantrell was involved in the scheme but to where was it to be removed? Chantrell wrote an account of the rebuilding which appeared in the *LI*, 4 Sept. 1841. In it he refers to the design as having gone through three stages; in the first of them the tower was to be removed 'to the north aisle', but does he mean the inner north aisle, adjacent to the nave and chancel, or the outer north aisle? Perhaps it was intended to be put over the inner aisle since in the 'second design' they would 'still keep the tower one bay north of the old one . . .'. Only in the 'last composition (which is now completed)' appeared the 'massive and highly ornamental tower which rises from the centre of the north front, at the end of the transept . . .'. This would seem to confirm that the positioning of the tower post-dated Chantrell's appointment.

The proposal to 'put new tracery into the windows' was, no doubt, Chantrell's. The poor state of the tracery had been commented on by Watson in his report of 1810 and the writer of *A Walk through Leeds* had also identified the windows as being especially ugly parts of the church. Thus the small rearrangement of the windows and the replacement of the tracery would have been a relatively easy way of giving the building a greater degree of dignity and a more 'ecclesiastical' appearance.

The winter of 1837–38 was taken up with detailed discussions between the building committee and its architect,[32] and in February 1838 tenders were invited for the 'renovation' of the eastern portion of the church.[33] At the same time, a letter to the *Intelligencer* from 'an old inhabitant' suggested an entirely new parish church should be built.[34] In answer to this a member of the building committee is quoted as saying this was quite out of the question and 'Mr Chantrell's plan for alterations had been unanimously adopted'.[35] In March the church was closed until the 'alterations' were complete,[36] and the workmen began to remove the monuments.[37] It was only then that the old structure could be fully examined and at this stage major problems were discovered.

> On the outer walls being opened and the roof and other woodwork being examined, the material was found to be more unsound and less available than was first calculated upon. As the works progressed and the wood casings round the stonework removed, the greater part of the building, together with the foundations, appeared in a most dangerous state,[38] particularly the tower, two of the piers which supported it being over weighted and cracked from top to bottom, their foundations were composed only of loose stones and rubbish, a little below the surface so that the tower could not be insured from day to day.[39]

[32] LPCA, 41/7: Building Committee Minute Book.
[33] *LI*, 17 Feb. 1838. It is interesting that the word 'renovation' rather than rebuilding is used.
[34] *Ibid.*, 24 Feb. 1838.
[35] *Ibid.*
[36] *LI*, 3 March 1838. It was expected that the church would reopen in 18 months.
[37] *LI*, 10 March 1838.
[38] Watson had warned of the very poor state of the foundations in the 1810 report.
[39] *LI*, 30 Nov. 1839.

Only two weeks after the member of the building committee had referred to the building being merely altered, a letter appeared in the *Intelligencer* from 'Dionysius' stating that, 'the south wall alone is to be retained, the remainder being razed to the foundations'.[40] In the same edition, tenders were invited for renovating not only the east end but the whole of the building.[41]

In April 1839 the *Intelligencer* was able to report that the 'rebuilding has progressed rapidly. The roof is putting onto the northern tower flat and the whole has already a very handsome appearance',[42] and in October of the same year the newspaper talked of 'the rapid progress now making towards completion of the new Parish Church with its noble tower'.[43] However, the total cost had risen from the intended £6,300, when work started in 1837, to £19,000 in 1839,[44] and an extra year was added to the expected length of time the work was to take,[45] as a result of the necessity virtually to rebuild the church. A meeting was called in November 1839, at which the vicar appealed for more funds. 'Bit by bit we found the church crumbling around us, and were placed in a predicament of building a new church, not repairing an old one[46] . . . when we found we should have to rebuild the church, we determined to do it substantially'.[47]

Two years later, at a similar meeting, the vicar gave more information about how the work on the church had proceeded, outlining the way in which it was rebuilt bit by bit, as further decay was found, and as further modifications seemed prudent. 'We had erected the west side of the church before the south side was

---

[40] *LI*, 10 March 1838. The architectural knowledge of the writer and the pseudonym – the Latin form of Chantrell's Christian name – suggests it was he who replied.

[41] The specification for the mason's work of March 1838 (ICBS unclassified papers at the Society of Antiquaries, London) gives a useful guide to the proposed work: '. . . when the foundations of the three lines of chancel pillars and great transept piers are finished, take down the clerestory and North and East walls as low as the foundations, raising the best of the said stone . . . the North transept must be taken down, the foundations examined on the sides . . . [alterations will also take place at] the Western end of the church . . .'.

[42] *LI*, 20 April 1839.

[43] *LI*, 26 Oct. 1839.

[44] *LI*, 30 Nov. 1839.

[45] *LI*, 21 April 1838. It was assumed then that the opening would be in the spring or summer of 1840.

[46] Some idea of the piecemeal reconstruction can be gained from the Building Accounts (LPCA, 41/5), which show the following payments for constructing the foundations: north transept, April 1838; north wall, May 1838; tower and north wall, June 1838; tower, June 1838; east end, July 1838; north and east pillars, July 1838; east end, October 1838; south transept, January 1839.

[47] *LI*, 30 Nov. 1839.

condemned; then, as we proceeded with the work, improvements suggested themselves, such as removing the organ from the north gallery to the south transept'.[48] It was on 21 January 1839 that the decision to move the organ was taken,[49] and, no doubt to accommodate it, the resolution was made to alter the south transept by extending it outwards by 10 feet.[50]

Various other ideas were examined during the course of the rebuilding. In July 1839, the building committee asked Chantrell to make a design for a 'western door under the large windows',[51] and in February 1840 there were discussions about vaulting the chancel.[52] But the most important modification to the original scheme was in the arrangement of the chancel, which will be discussed later.

As the building neared completion, regular accounts of progress appeared in the local newspapers: 'The work is proceeding rapidly and some idea may now be formed of what the beautiful structure will look like when finished . . .'[53] In October 1840, the *Intelligencer* even went so far as to state that the church would be 'one of the most splendid parochial churches in the Kingdom'. In May 1841, the finishing touches were being applied to the interior. 'We understand that carpenters, plasterers etc will finish the body of the church in about 10 days. The painting will take about one month, and a further month is allowed for drying and cleaning. The stained glass windows are nearly ready.'[54] At the last minute, it was found necessary to remove the whole of the elegant stone tracery in the belfry window and replace it with louvre boards, as it concealed the full effect of the newly installed peal of bells.[55]

Eventually, 2 September 1841 was announced as the date of the consecration,[56] more than four years after the first proposals were put forward, and after £30,000 had been spent on the project, five times the original estimate. However, there was no suggestion of criticism of Chantrell for overspending or underestimating. In fact he was praised for the way in which he was able to work in this 'piecemeal' manner: 'In nothing was the genius of the architect more

---

[48] *LI*, 23 Oct. 1841.
[49] LPCA, 41/8: Building Committee Minute Book.
[50] *Ibid.* There were various discussions of it in Jan., May and June 1839.
[51] *Ibid.*
[52] LPCA, 41/7: Building Committee Minute Book, 17 Feb. 1840.
[53] *LI*, 4 April 1840.
[54] *LI*, 1 May 1841.
[55] *LI*, 8 May 1841.
[56] *LI*, 31 July 1841. It had been postponed from 11 August as the Archbishop of York wished to be present: *LI*, 24 July 1841.

strikingly displayed than in the skill with which Mr Chantrell availed himself of the circumstances as they occurred. What would have perplexed an architect of fewer resources was only, for him, an opportunity of evincing his power . . .'.[57] Two years earlier, at a public meeting, the vicar offered similar praise: 'It is quite impossible for me to speak in terms sufficiently to show the skill and genius exhibited in this great work by our architect, Mr Chantrell . . .'.[58] When it was finished the town was suitably impressed by its new church and more than satisfied with its architect. There was, too, a deserved self-satisfaction for the parishioners as the *Intelligencer's* report of the consecration makes clear:

> We owe this beautiful edifice to the ardent zeal of the Vicar, Dr Hook, and the liberality and devotion of the churches of Leeds and the immediate neighbourhood. The means placed at the disposal of Mr Chantrell, the able architect, precluded him from doing all he wished, but, looking at those means, and many restrictions under which he unavoidably laboured by being compelled to adhere to the site of the old edifice, it must be admitted that he has done wonders, and raised a monument to his own fame, as well as a temple to the Almighty . . . Taken as a whole, the Parish Church of Leeds may be pronounced one of the finest, if not the finest in the Kingdom. All the internal arrangements are admirable; the 'tout ensemble' brilliant. It is truly an honour to Leeds; and those who have contributed to the work ought to consider it as one of the privileges of their lives . . .[59]

By the time of its completion, 'the whole [church had] been taken down and rebuilt, with the exception of a portion of the south wall. A new south entrance porch is erected, the south transept has been extended twelve feet, the chancel extended eastwards on the site of the old vestry . . .'[60]

It was probably when it was first realised that part of the structure would have to be rebuilt that Chantrell decided to use the style 'of the latter part of the fourteenth century',[61] in order harmonise with the rest of the old building which it was anticipated would survive. Chantrell described the architecture of this period as generally being a

[57] *LI*, 23 Oct. 1841.
[58] *LI*, 30 Nov. 1839.
[59] *LI*, 4 Sept. 1841.
[60] *LI*, 28 Aug. 1841.
[61] *Ibid.*

transition from the Decorated to the Perpendicular style, which has its peculiarities, though unnoticed by modern writers on Gothic architecture, and admits of a variety of forms which the others do not; the masses partake more generally of the decorated character, but the flowing arch of the minuter parts terminates gracefully in the vertical tracery of the windows, and where no tracery is above it, finials form the termination of the cusped arches of the transoms: after this the whole forms become Perpendicular, and in the fifteenth century the style was nearly abandoned.[62]

Perhaps more importantly, it was a period in which such features as the windows had been sufficiently varied to give Chantrell the flexibility which he needed in such an irregular building. For instance the north wall had to be low enough to let light pass over the outer north aisle roof, and into the clerestory of the inner north aisle, which in turn had to be low enough to let light pass over it and into the clerestory of the nave (Plate 28(b)). Consequently, pointed windows in the north wall, or in either of these two clerestories were ruled out,[63] and Chantrell had to use rectangular windows made up of two or three lights. In contrast, the south side had no such problems since a single aisle allowed for a much higher outer wall.[64] In it, Chantrell placed a series of narrow pointed windows,[65] filled with elegant Perpendicular tracery (Plate 28(a)).

G. W. O. Addleshaw and F. Etchells were quite clear about the significance of Leeds Parish Church: 'architecturally it is not important; but in plan and arrangement it is epoch making, being the first large town church to exemplify the principles of the Cambridge ecclesiologists'.[66] One might take exception to their view of its architectural importance since the plan was largely what was inherited from the old church but it is true that the internal arrangement was revolutionary. It was probably from his friend

---

[62] *Ibid.*

[63] Subsequently, Chantrell claimed that he would have specified pointed arches, had more money been available: see below, pp. 140, 146.

[64] However, the clerestory still has low, rectangular windows, but these are almost hidden from the outside.

[65] Chantrell perhaps felt the windows added sufficient verticality, and to save money, used much simpler buttresses which are without pinnacles.

[66] G. W. O. Addleshaw, and F. Etchells, *The Architectural Setting of Anglican Worship* (1948), p.211. This work presents a thorough account of Leeds Parish Church in the context of the development of Anglican worship on pp. 203–22.

John Jebb, canon of Hereford and an influential commentator on liturgical reform, that Hook had come to appreciate the disadvantages of a screen between the nave and chancel of a large cruciform church or cathedral which denied the congregation a view of the altar and celebrant. In his earliest scheme for altering the church, Hook proposed not only to remove the screen and organ gallery but, by widening the crossing piers, he intended further to strengthen the visual bond between the congregation and the altar. However, in this first plan, much of the chancel was to be filled with pews; only later did this part of the church take on its 'epoch making' form. The 1837 plans which accompanied the faculty show that three of the four bays of the chancel were to contain seats for the congregation, leaving only the eastern bay for the sanctuary; the north and south galleries were intended to run the full length of the chancel and abut the east wall. It would have been an arrangement that differed little in principle from most other churches of the period.

As built, the altar is situated in a canted bay extending eastwards approximately the width of one of the chancel bays. The chancel was left almost entirely free of pews for the congregation, with the only pews east of the crossing being in the first one and a half bays of the chancel aisles. In the chancel proper, the first bay was to be taken up with choir stalls, and the three eastern bays left quite empty. Furthermore, the importance of the altar was emphasised by no less than seven steps leading to it, and the north and south galleries extending only into the first two bays of the chancel aisles (Plate 29(a)).

The executed plan was, in a number of ways, in accord with principles of the ecclesiologists but, as Addleshaw and Etchells have pointed out, there are two additional features, 'due not to the ecclesiologists, but to Jebb and Hook himself. Before the communion rail is a wide step where communicants can kneel from the Invitation onwards . . . the other feature is the presence in the choir stalls of a lay surpliced choir . . .'.[67] The former is thought to have been Hook's idea but the latter originated in a request from the parishioners to which 'Hook not overwillingly agreed'. He enlisted Jebb's help in forming a choir and no doubt Jebb also influenced its placing within the church.[68] It was only on 17 August 1840 that the building committee resolved to modify the arrangement of the chancel and

[67] *Ibid.*, pp.212–13.
[68] *Ibid.*, Jebb had a deep interest in cathedral choirs, including the arrangement of their stalls.

incorporate the choir stalls, altar rail and the steps leading to the sanctuary.[69]

It would be reasonable to assume that Chantrell left to Hook details of planning which were essentially liturgical. However it is possible to detect a classical basis to the plan which could have been Chantrell's contribution to Hook's desire for a dignified interior. There are two axes, north-south and east-west; there is an impression of symmetry about both of them; views along these axes have a visual feature at their termination. Furthermore, the manipulation of space – best experienced by walking from the north entrance through the narrow but tall north transept, then experiencing the vastness of nave and chancel but still not seeing the altar until one turns through ninety degrees in the centre of the crossing – follows the tradition of late eighteenth-century classicism in which Chantrell had been educated. In other respects the interior is a compromise and is less successful for it. Kenneth Powell has noted perceptively that 'one feels that the church is almost two separate compartments – the nave for preaching (Plate 29(b)), and the long steadily rising east end for the sacrament of the altar . . .'.[70] It was the nave, with galleries on three sides in the 'Commissioners' manner, which precluded the church from being fully approved of by later critics. But there was no other way to accommodate a large congregation, and the value of the galleries increased as less of the chancel came to be available for the congregation in successive stages of the scheme of rebuilding. Chantrell was well aware of the problem and admitted that 'galleries in churches are at all times defects; thus they are supported by small iron pillars, placed behind, and independent of, the stone pillars which support the clerestory and roof, to denote that they, like pews, are mere furniture'.[71] The ceiling is another aspect of the design that is 'incorrect' in an archaeological sense, and not consistent throughout the building. Again Chantrell recognised the problems:

> In ancient Churches stone groined arches covered the building, but the walls were required to be of great thickness, as well as the pillars that supported them, and buttresses were carried across the side aisles to counteract their pressure. These groins can now only be represented by timber and plaster, unless at an enormous expense. Open roofs of plain timbers were common in the lesser

[69] LPCA, 41/7; Building Committee Minute Book.
[70] K. Powell, 'Victorian Church Triumphant', *Country Life* (20 Dec. 1984), p. 1968.
[71] *LI*, 4 Sept. 1841.

> churches, but we can scarcely associate ideas of comfort
> with them, any more than in the dress worn five centuries
> ago. This latter effect is in some degree preserved by
> showing the timbers of the roof enriched, and the space
> between them covered with oak boarding, to conceal
> the slates.[72]

Twenty years later he was to reflect: 'My church at Leeds is but imperfect: but, had I been unlimited, the clerestory windows would have had pointed arches, and the open roof of oak, enriched with tracery . . .'[73] But at the time of its completion few people would have been concerned about such relatively minor matters. Indeed the consecration was considered so important an event that 'the opening was delayed slightly as the Archbishop of York was anxious to be present',[74] and at the service he was accompanied by three bishops and about three hundred clergymen.[75] The building became influential even outside England; the sermon at the consecration was preached by George Washington Doane, bishop of New Jersey, and the second American bishop to be elected a member of the Cambridge Camden Society.[76] While in England, he made an extensive tour of cathedrals and churches, but St Peter's represented, for him, an ideal model for the American churches.[77] St Peter's also influenced the design of Christ Church, St Lawrence, Sydney. That building was begun in 1840 but finished by Edmund Blacket, an architect with Yorkshire connections, who arrived there in 1845. In his revised design, the seating and choir were arranged on the model of St Peter's, Leeds.[78]

Pugin approved of the asymmetry of the new St Peter's, abhorring 'the present regular system of building both sides of the church alike'.[79] The *Ecclesiologist* had its criticisms of the building but acknowledged that 'it is the first great instance . . . of the Catholic feeling of a church, energising rudimentally – throwing off, by a strong, vigorous mental effort, the mere preaching house, grasping at the altar as being, rather than the pulpit, the central point of

[72] *Ibid.*

[73] *Builder*, XIX (1861), p.778.

[74] *LI*, 24 July 1841.

[75] *Ecclesiologist*, VIII (1847), p.132.

[76] P. Stanton, *The Gothic Revival and American Church Architecture* (Baltimore, 1968), p.32.

[77] *Ibid.*

[78] Linstrum, p.217. Blacket was also connected with the planning of St Andrew's, Sydney, which showed the influence of Leeds Parish Church.

[79] A. W. M. Pugin, *The Present State . . .* (1843), p.22.

worship . . .'.[80] The movement which this magazine represented saw it as 'the first large town church to exemplify [its] principles'.[81] The new Leeds Parish Church, with its unique internal arrangement,[82] and Hook with his advanced ideas concerning the liturgy,[83] were held in special regard by many of the members of the more 'progressive' wing of the Church of England. However, despite the initial widespread approval of the church, its direct influence on Gothic Revival in England was negligible. New churches were not built on the model of Chantrell's St Peter's, and only six years after its consecration the *Ecclesiologist* felt its architectural significance had long passed.

> [It] can now only be studied as an historical monument'. It had certainly been important as the first great instance . . . of the catholic feeling of a church . . . and yet [it had] not been able to compass those points of church arrangement which are the result of study and patient research . . . [It is not] a Protestant preaching-hall; nor . . . a church as we should like to build . . . There is no ritual chancel, strictly speaking, but rather a chorus cantorum, stalls being arranged up the alley of the eastern limb . . .[84]

Alongside this criticism, in the same article the writer went on to praise J. M. Derrick's St Saviour's, Leeds, begun the year after St Peter's was finished, which he saw as a 'more mature' example of the then current church movement. 'The interior is extremely impressive and religious; more so, it struck us than that of any modern church we had ever yet seen.' The writer uses St Saviour's

[80] *Ecclesiologist*, VIII (1847), p.132.
[81] Addleshaw and Etchells, p.211.
[82] The *Ecclesiologist* saw it as 'the first large church with a Catholic feeling', *Ecclesiologist*, VIII (1847), p.132.
[83] But at no time since the rebuilding of the parish church has its worship shown any Anglo-Catholic tendencies. When, in the later years of the nineteenth century, Anglican worship moved in a Catholic direction, Leeds Parish Church worship patterns were unaltered, and it became a stronghold of the Broad Church movement. Hence the well-known local saying, 'There's high church and low church and Leeds Parish Church' – suggesting, not without some justification, that the church's ritual was something peculiar to itself.
[84] *Ecclesiologist*, VIII (1847), p.132.

and St Peter's to some extent, as examples of what good modern churches ought and ought not to be respectively. While St Peter's was seen as an important improvement on the churches of the earlier nineteenth century, it failed to conform to the *Ecclesiologist's* somewhat narrow view of what a sound, modern plan should be.

CHAPTER 6

Epilogue: Chantrell in the South of England, 1847–1872

An official announcement of Chantrell's move from Leeds to London appeared in the *Leeds Intelligencer*, 2 January 1847, and gave his 'new' address as 21 Lincoln's Inn Fields. However he was not living exclusively at *Oatlands* prior to this date as he owned, or rented, the Lincoln's Inn Fields house at least as early as September 1845,[1] and various references exist which confirm stays in London from the early 1840s. Although Chantrell cited Lincoln's Inn Fields as his professional address, his removal to London marked his virtual retirement from the practice of architecture. No important commission has come to light which might have explained his departure from Leeds, aged only fifty-four and at the peak of his career. After 1847 his limited professional employment mainly involved completing churches started before he left Leeds or altering buildings which he had designed much earlier. For example, he undertook the restoration of the west gable and bell turret of All Saints, Netherthong, after storm damage in 1847 (Plate 30(a)) and in 1844–49 he added a channel to Emmanuel church, Lockwood (Plate 30(b)). Both these churches had originally been built to Chantrell's designs in the 1820s. Chantrell was also involved in the rebuilding of Fangfoss church (E. Riding) (1849–50) and the church at Peasenhall, Suffolk (*c.*1858), and in alterations to St Michael's, Malton (N. Riding) (*c.*1849–50).

Chantrell's choice of a London house in such proximity to Soane's former office, at this time already part of the Sir John Soane's Museum, could suggest merely a harking back to the period of his pupilage. Alternatively it might betray an ambition to achieve for

[1] On 3 September 1845 he wrote to the CBC from this address: CBC, Leeds, St Philip's, file no. 20547. Messrs Chantrell continued to have an office in Leeds until at least 1851: W. Slade and D. I. Roebuck, *Slade and Roebuck's Directory of the Borough and Neighbourhood of Leeds* (Leeds, 1851) p.467, and J. B. Chantrell is recorded as being in practice on his own in 1853: W. White *Directory and Gazetteer of Leeds* (Leeds, 1853) p.61. However, there is no evidence to suggest that John sought or received any new commissions for either practice.

the Gothic Revival what Soane had for the Classical. After all, for a brief period in the mid 1840s, after the death of Thomas Rickman but before the next generation of architects, including George Gilbert Scott and William Butterfield, were fully established, there can have been few men to equal Chantrell's knowledge of Gothic architecture. Perhaps the most plausible explanation for Chantrell's retirement from practice, however, is that on reaching a position at which he no longer needed the income from his practice, maybe as a result of inheritance, he now sought to carve out an influential role for himself as an 'elder statesman' within the architectural establishment. Certainly the known facts of his first years in London suggest this.

On 3 May 1847 Chantrell was elected an ordinary member of the council of the Institute of British Architects[2] and on 14 June he read to the institute his paper on 'The Geometric System . . .'. The review of this in the *Gentleman's Magazine*[3] and the detailed explanations of the system which appeared in the *Builder*[4] served to publicise further his contribution to the study of the subject. In 1850 he exhibited at the Free Architects' Exhibition,[5] but perhaps it was the damning though unsubstantiated criticism to which his drawings were subjected in the *Ecclesiologist* that dissuaded him from exhibiting subsequently.

Meanwhile, however, Chantrell's position was enhanced through his involvement with the Incorporated Church Building Society. In February 1848 the Society's committee resolved to reform its method of inspection of church buildings by instituting 'a system whereby architects were appointed to inspect plans and works', the costs for this being charged to the applicants who submitted designs. A committee of architects was set up, meeting for the first time on 2 March 1848. Present were Anthony Salvin, Benjamin Ferry, T. H. Wyatt, J. H. Hakewill, J. P. Harrison, Richard Carpenter, Raphael Brandon and J. Clarke.[6] The eight, with G. G. Scott, were divided into three groups of three architects. Each trio was to meet three

[2] *Gentleman's Magazine*, XXVIII (1847), pt ii, p.67.
[3] *Ibid.*, pp.68–69.
[4] *Builder*, V (1847), pp.300–02. Also in 1847, he read a paper to the IBA on the 'Norman Roof of Adel Church'.
[5] *Ecclesiologist*, XI (1850), p.174. Exhibit number 136 was a drawing of his new church at Armitage Bridge which the journal described as 'absolutely wretched', and number 169 was a view of his additions to Bruges Cathedral which the reviewer thought were '. . . a portentous mass of bastard Romanesque frippery [which were] ruinous to the tower'.
[6] ICBS, Committee of Architects Minute Book, 1848–1958.

times a year, giving a total of nine meetings at which plans could be submitted for inspection by parishes wishing to secure a grant from the Society. In addition to attending these meetings, each architect was given a geographical area of the country within which he was to be responsible for inspecting buildings in progress.

The committee of architects meeting of 31 March 1849 decided to carry these arrangements further: they proposed that three additional architects be appointed – Chantrell, Ewan Christian and David Brandon – and that the twelve should be divided into three groups of four to meet in rotation to inspect plans, etc. Chantrell was given the superintendence of the 'Diocese of York'.[7] The minute book gives little detail of what was discussed at meetings but it records that Chantrell attended meetings diligently for the next fourteen years in the company of some of the country's leading ecclesiastical architects.

The committee had resolved not to supply plans for churches in England so as not to out-do fellow professionals, but it was prepared willingly to give free advice on such matters as restorations and erections.[8] This would seem to account for Chantrell's involvement with work at Fangfoss church and St Michael's, Malton. Both churches had been built in the twelfth century and this required a sympathetic architectural treatment. As they were situated in Yorkshire, they would have been known to Chantrell had their wardens approached the ICBS for a grant,[9] or merely advice.

It was while the church at Peasenhall (Suffolk) was being built that 'renovations' and 'improvements' were again taking place at Leeds Parish Church. The *Builder* reported that the work included cleaning, repainting and revarnishing. Also, 'the capitals of the columns have been recarved, and the foliage deepened; . . . the niches in the arch of the great chancel window have been filled with Caen stone figures of the four Evangelists, . . . the floor of the chancel has been relayed . . . the window sills have been cut about 8 inches lower . . .' and new stained glass windows had been inserted in some of the windows.[10] It was, perhaps, through this journal that Chantrell learned of the changes and, despite the passing of twenty years since its opening, he was clearly indignant that his most important building had to be altered without his sanction. He wrote

[7] *Ibid.*; perhaps his area also contained the recently formed Diocese of Ripon.

[8] *Ibid.*, 31 March 1849.

[9] No record can be found in the ICBS papers of a grant application form from either parish.

[10] *Builder*, XIX (1861), p.621.

to the *Builder* pointing out that much of what had recently been done either had had little effect on the appearance of the interior or was only what he himself would have wished to do had attitudes to church decoration not been so conservative at the time the church was built. More importantly, Chantrell showed that even by this late stage in his career he still attached importance to the professional integrity which, no doubt, Soane had instilled in him. He concluded his letter:

> . . . What would the architect of the Royal Exchange say, if some young Tyro, even though patronized for a worthy father's name only, were allowed to thus desecrate the Royal Exchange? Or the architect of Doncaster New Church, were a Tudor window substituted for one of his, by the kotooing to Mammon of unscrupulous wardens of that fine work? Reared in a noble school of architecture, I would not have dared, during nearly half a century of practice, to have thus intruded myself upon the work of any living brother professor. My church at Leeds is but imperfect; but, had I been unlimited, the clerestory windows would have had pointed arches, and the open roof of oak, enriched with tracery, and colouring wherewith to harmonize the tout-ensemble; and the sedilia, with several embellishments, intended, but left undone, would have enabled me to produce a work in 1840 which I could revisit, after twenty years' absence, with satisfaction. Why should we talk of international copyright, if our works are in our own country permitted to be mutilated? Independently of my profession, courtesy, in some degree at least, I claim.[11]

Although not named in this letter, E. M. Barry, who had 'revised a design' for one of the windows, published a reply defending his actions.[12] Chantrell's reply to Barry's letter concluded with a remark which suggests that St Peter's was by no means the only one of his churches which had been subject to subsequent alterations of which he did not approve:

> . . . After a lapse of twenty years I was not aware that a living architect should feel no interest in a completed

[11] *Ibid.*, p.778.
[12] *Ibid.*, p.792.

work when committed to the 'conservation' of churchwardens who, by the by, are noted for their beautifying
of churches, though mostly in defiance of taste,
judgement, or the most remote sense of propriety: 'ne
sutor ultra crepidam'.[13]

The year 1863 was a difficult one for Chantrell. On 9 February
his wife died,[14] just three days before their forty-ninth wedding
anniversary. Chantrell's own health was not good and perhaps it
was this, in addition to his bereavement, which prompted him to
move to the more salubrious atmosphere of the south coast. By
31 May 1863 he was living temporarily at Meads House, Eastbourne,
and on that date wrote to the secretary of the ICBS architects
committee offering an apology on medical grounds for his absence
from their forthcoming annual dinner. At the Annual Meeting on
3 June, which Chantrell did not attend, it was proposed that 'as
R. D. Chantrell is now in Eastbourne it would be better if he
resigned as one of the London Committee of Architects and become
an Honorary Member, but quite exceptionally, he can still keep his
surveyorship of the Ripon Diocese if he wishes'. In a letter to the
Society Chantrell regretted his enforced departure and hinted at a
feeling of bitterness that he, as one of the most consistent attenders,
should have been voted out at almost the first meeting he missed.
An objective reading of the minutes suggests that the committee
acted with undue haste in assuming that he would be unable to
discharge his duties. Chantrell was now seventy years of age and
probably the oldest member of the committee: perhaps the more
dynamic younger members, especially those in whom the more
advanced ecclesiastical sympathies predominated, found him difficult
to deal with and welcomed the opportunity to remove him from
office. This would seem to mark the end of his active contact with
architecture, although he continued his membership of the Institute
of British Architects until 1868.[15]

In 1864 Chantrell settled in Rottingdean, near Brighton,[16] and
remained there until his death on 4 January 1872. The place of his
burial is not known and no obituary appears to have been written.
Some four years before his death he had married for a second time.

---

[13] *Ibid.*, p.812.
[14] City of Bruges Public Records, register of marriages, 1884, no.260. This records
the marriage of R. D. Chantrell (junior) to Mary Dryancour, and includes details
of the bridegroom's parents.
[15] RIBA Library, Index of Members.
[16] *Ibid.*

Even before Chantrell's death, many of his buildings had become unfashionable and some had been subjected to 'improvements'.[17] When Rusby's mammoth work on Leeds Parish Church appeared in 1896, it is significant that Chantrell's name appeared only once.[18] More recently, there were few protests when his Christ Church, Leeds, was demolished and the disappearance of his schools at Holbeck and Hunslet, bulldozed within a few days of each other in 1978, went unnoticed. St Matthew's, Holbeck, is threatened with demolition and Chantrell's only identified house, Armitage Bridge House, for many years derelict, has now been subjected to an insensitive modernisation.

However, the future of many of Chantrell's churches is more secure, even if the name of their designer is known to few. Ironically, these buildings are valued not primarily because their interiors are now regarded as well planned, or because their details are seen as the product of archaeological scholarship, but because they are such important elements in the townscapes of which they form a part. Keighley, Honley and Cowling are obvious examples. The status of Leeds Parish Church, cut off as it is from the city centre by the railway, has been the subject of debate in recent years, but, with the recent reorganisation of ecclesiastical provision in the city, its role in the religious and civic life of Leeds now seems more assured. The recent adaptation of part of the outer north aisle to form the 'City of Leeds Room' subsequently has been an important factor in the revitalisation of the building and the newly cleaned exterior has enabled Chantrell's 'great undertaking' to be fully appreciated. His obscurity during the last hundred years has, to some extent, been redressed by the naming of the newly erected flats to the south-east of the Parish Church 'Chantrell Court'.

[17] For instance the Philosophical and Literary Hall in Leeds was extended and given a more 'Italianate' quality by C. R. Chorley in 1861–62; St Stephen's, Kirkstall, had a long chancel and transepts added in 1863; his churches at Hunslet and Bramley had been demolished.

[18] Rusby, *Parish Church*, p.73.

APPENDIX
Catalogue of Chantrell's Commissions

Readers requiring more information about the commissions listed below are directed to Webster, Appendix 2, which contains comprehensive entries for each scheme, including a list of sources.

Unless stated otherwise, the following commissions were for new buildings:

ADEL, NR LEEDS:	St John Baptist.
	Rebuilt west gable and bellcote, 1838–39.
	Re-roofed chancel, 1843.
ARMITAGE BRIDGE, NR HUDDERSFIELD:	Armitage Bridge House. 1828.
ARMITAGE BRIDGE:	St Paul. c.1844–48.
ARMITAGE BRIDGE:	School. 1835 (attributed).
ARMITAGE BRIDGE:	Vicarage. c.1845–48 (attributed).
ARMLEY, LEEDS:	Almshouses and School. 1832 (attributed), demolished.
ARMLEY:	Chapel. Extension, 1823–25, demolished.
	Alterations and extension, 1833–34, demolished.
	Proposed alterations, 1844.
BAKEWELL, DERBYSHIRE:	All Saints.
	Unexecuted design for internal remodelling, c. 1830.
BATLEY CARR, WR:	Holy Trinity, 1839.
BIRKENSHAW, WR:	St Paul's. Repairs, 1835.
BIRSTWITH, NR HARROGATE:	Unidentified house. 1840.
BRAMLEY, LEEDS:	Chapel. New belfry, 1821, demolished.
	Unexecuted design for enlargement, 1822.
	Unexecuted design for a new chapel, 1824.
	Unexecuted design for a new chapel, 1828.
	Alterations and extension, 1833, demolished.
BRAMLEY:	Parsonage. 1823.
BRUGES, BELGIUM:	Cathedral of St Saviour.
	Restoration of roof following a fire, and addition to the tower, 1839–46.
CHAPEL ALLERTON, LEEDS:	St Matthew.
	Alterations, 1839–41, demolished.
CLECKHEATON, WR:	St John. Repairs, 1840.
COWLING, NR SKIPTON:	Holy Trinity. c.1839–1845.
DENHOLME GATE, NR HALIFAX:	St Paul. 1843–46.
DEWSBURY:	All Saints, Monument to Mrs Abbott. 1843.
DEWSBURY:	Church of England School. c.1842.
DEWSBURY:	St John. Repairs, 1839–40.
EARLSHEATON, DEWSBURY:	St Peter. Repairs, c.1840, demolished.
EAST ARDSLEY, WR:	St Michael. Unexecuted design for rebuilding, 1843–44.
FANGFOSS, ER:	St Martin. Rebuilt church, c.1849–50.
FARNLEY TYAS, NR HUDDERSFIELD:	St Lucius. 1838–40.
GLOSSOP, DERBYSHIRE:	All Saints. Restoration, 1827–c.32.
GOLCAR, WR:	St John. Repairs, 1842–44.
GUISELEY, WR:	St Oswald. Alterations, 1830–33.
HALIFAX:	King Cross Chapel. Survey and report, 1826.
HALIFAX:	St John. Repairs, c.1818–20.
HALIFAX:	St Paul. 1844–47, demolished, except for tower and spire.
HARROGATE:	Baths for the Poor. Unexecuted design, 1821.
HEADINGLEY, LEEDS:	St Michael. 1836–38, demolished.

HEADINGLEY:	Unidentified house. 1842.
HECKMONDWIKE, WR:	St James. Repairs, 1840.
HEMSWORTH, WR:	St Helen. Restoration of chancel, 1842, (?) unexecuted.
HOLBECK, LEEDS:	St Matthew. 1827–32.
HOLBECK:	School. 1840, demolished.
HOLMBRIDGE, WR:	St David. Unexecuted design for new church, 1837.
HONLEY, NR HUDDERSFIELD:	Old Chapel. Survey and report, 1830.
HONLEY:	St Mary. 1840–44.
HUNSLET, LEEDS:	St Mary. Internal alterations, 1826, demolished. New tower, 1830–31, demolished. Alterations, 1843–44, demolished.
HUNSLET:	School. c.1840–43, demolished.
HYDE, CHESHIRE:	St George. Unexecuted design for new church, 1828.
KEIGHLEY:	St Andrew. 1845–48.
KIRKSTALL, LEEDS:	Chapel. Unexecuted design, c.1820.
KIRKSTALL:	Parsonage. 1834–35, demolished.
KIRKSTALL:	St Stephen. 1827–29. Repairs to spire, 1833.
LEEDS:	Central Market. Unexecuted design, 1824.
LEEDS:	Christ Church. 1821–26 demolished. Alterations, 1828, demolished. New perimeter wall, 1829, demolished. New north and south galleries, 1836, demolished. Repairs, 1839, demolished.
LEEDS:	Christ Church, School. c.1839–42, demolished.
LEEDS:	Clarendon Rd, Atkinson estate. Unexecuted design for gatelodge, 1838.
LEEDS:	Commercial Buildings. Unsuccessful competition entry, 1825.
LEEDS:	Conservative Pavilion. 1838, temporary structure.
LEEDS:	Court House. Alterations, 1840–41, demolished.
LEEDS:	Drying house in or near Meadow Lane. New building, or survey of existing building, 1819, presumed demolished.
LEEDS:	Free School. New perimeter wall, 1824, demolished. Repairs, 1825, demolished.
LEEDS:	General Cemetery. Unsuccessful competition entry, 1833.
LEEDS:	Holy Trinity. Repairs and addition of upper section of tower, 1839. Repairs, 1841–42.
LEEDS:	Library. New east gallery, 1821. Alterations, 1828. Alterations, 1835.
LEEDS:	Philosophical and Literary Society Hall. 1819–21, demolished. Unexecuted scheme for alterations, 1826. Alterations, 1839–40, demolished. Design of pedestal for statue of J. M. Sadler, 1843.

LEEDS:	Music Hall.
	Alterations, 1821, demolished.
	Alterations, 1824–25, demolished.
	Alterations, 1840, demolished.
LEEDS:	Oratory. 1838, demolished.
LEEDS:	Public Baths. 1819–21, demolished.
LEEDS:	St George.
	Unexecuted design for new church, 1836.
LEEDS:	St John.
	Repairs and alterations, 1838.
LEEDS:	St Mark.
	Internal alterations, 1827.
	Minor works, 1827–28.
	New west gallery, 1832–34.
	New south gallery, 1836–37, removed.
	New organ screen, 1838.
LEEDS:	St Mark, School, Feather Hill.
	Enlargement, 1832, demolished.
LEEDS:	St Mary.
	Laying out of new burial ground, 1829.
LEEDS:	St Mary, School. c.1829.
LEEDS:	St Peter. Rebuilding, 1837–41.
	Monument to Ralph Thoresby, c.1841.
LEEDS:	St Philip.
	1845–47, demolished.
LEEDS:	St Philip, School.
	Extension, 1843, demolished.
LEEDS:	Shops in Bond Street. 1820.
LEEDS:	South Market.
	1823–24, demolished.
LEEDS:	Unidentified house. 1825.
LEEDS:	Unidentified houses in Woodhouse Lane. 1842.
LEEDS:	Vicarage (6 Park Place). Repairs, 1826.
LEEDS:	Yorkshire Agricultural Society Pavilion. 1839, temporary structure.
LEVEN, ER:	Holy Trinity. 1840–45.
LOCKWOOD, NR HUDDERSFIELD:	Emmanuel. 1826–30.
	New chancel, 1848–49.
LOTHERSDALE, NR SKIPTON:	Christ Church. 1837–38.
LUND, ER:	All Saints. Rebuilt chancel, 1845–46.
MALTON, NR:	St Michael. New chancel, 1858.
MIDDLETON, LEEDS:	St Mary. 1845–46.
MIDDLETON, LEEDS:	St Mary, Vicarage.
	c.1845–49, demolished.
MORLEY, NR LEEDS:	National District School. 1832 (attributed).
MORLEY:	St Peter. 1828–30.
NETHERTHONG, WR:	All Saints. 1826–30.
	Repairs and new bell turret, 1847.
NEW MILLS, DERBYSHIRE:	St George. 1827–31.
PEASENHALL, SUFFOLK:	St Michael. Rebuilt church, 1860–61.
PONTEFRACT:	All Saints. Restoration, 1831–33.
POOL, NR OTLEY:	St Wilfrid. 1838–40.
RISE, ER:	All Saints. 1844.
ROBERTTOWN, WR:	All Saints. 1843.
RUDDING PARK, NR HARROGATE:	Alterations and repairs, after 1824–c.1835.
SHADWELL, NR LEEDS:	St Paul. 1840–42.
SKIPTON, WR:	Christ Church. 1835–39.
UNIDENTIFIED LOCATION:	Design for a residence and garden, 1822.
WORTLEY, LEEDS:	Unidentified house. 1844.

Index

(Page-numbers in italic denote illustrations)